HEART LAMP

Lamp of Mahamudra

&

The Heart of the Matter

Rangjung Yeshe Books ❖ www.rangjung.com

PADMASAMBHAVA ❖ *Treasures from Juniper Ridge* ❖ *Advice from the Lotus-Born* ❖ *Dakini Teachings*

PADMASAMBHAVA AND JAMGÖN KONGTRÜL ❖ *The Light of Wisdom, Vol. 1* ❖ *The Light of Wisdom, Vol. 2*

YESHE TSOGYAL ❖ *The Lotus-Born*

GAMPOPA ❖ *The Precious Garland of the Sublime Path*

DAKPO TASHI NAMGYAL ❖ *Clarifying the Natural State*

TSELE NATSOK RANGDRÖL ❖ *Mirror of Mindfulness* ❖ *Empowerment* ❖ *Heart Lamp*

CHOKGYUR LINGPA ❖ *Ocean of Amrita* ❖ *The Great Gate* ❖ *Skillful Grace*

JAMGÖN MIPHAM RINPOCHE ❖ *Gateway to Knowledge, Vol. 1, Vol. 2, & Vol. 3*

TULKU URGYEN RINPOCHE ❖ *Blazing Splendor* ❖ *Rainbow Painting* ❖ *As It Is, Vol. 1* ❖ *As It Is, Vol. 2* ❖ *Vajra Speech* ❖ *Repeating the Words of the Buddha*

KHENCHEN THRANGU RINPOCHE ❖ *Crystal Clear* ❖ *Songs of Naropa* ❖ *King of Samadhi* ❖ *Buddha Nature*

CHÖKYI NYIMA RINPOCHE ❖ *Present Fresh Wakefulness* ❖ *Indisputable Truth* ❖ *Union of Mahamudra & Dzogchen* ❖ *Bardo Guidebook* ❖ *Song of Karmapa*

TSIKEY CHOKLING RINPOCHE ❖ *Lotus Ocean*

TULKU THONDUP ❖ *Enlightened Living*

ORGYEN TOBGYAL RINPOCHE ❖ *Life & Teachings of Chokgyur Lingpa*

DZIGAR KONGTRÜL ❖ *Uncommon Happiness*

TSOKNYI RINPOCHE ❖ *Fearless Simplicity* ❖ *Carefree Dignity*

DZOGCHEN TRILOGY COMPILED BY MARCIA BINDER SCHMIDT ❖ *Dzogchen Primer* ❖ *Dzogchen Essentials* ❖ *Quintessential Dzogchen*

ERIK PEMA KUNSANG ❖ *Wellsprings of the Great Perfection* ❖ *A Tibetan Buddhist Companion* ❖ *The Rangjung Yeshe Tibetan-English Dictionary of Buddhist Culture*

HEART LAMP

Lamp of Mahamudra

THE IMMACULATE LAMP THAT PERFECTLY AND FULLY
ILLUMINATES THE MEANING OF MAHAMUDRA,
THE ESSENCE OF ALL PHENOMENA

The Heart of the Matter

THE UNCHANGING CONVERGENCE OF VITAL POINTS
THAT SHOWS EXACTLY HOW TO APPLY THE VIEW AND
MEDITATION OF THE DEFINITIVE MEANING

Tsele Natsok Rangdrol

Foreword by Dilgo Khyentse Rinpoche
Introductions by Tulku Urgyen Rinpoche &
Chökyi Nyima Rinpoche
Translated by Erik Pema Kunsang

RANGJUNG YESHE PUBLICATIONS
BOUDHANATH, HONG KONG & ESBY
2009

Rangjung Yeshe Publications
Flat 5a, Greenview Garden,
125 Robinson Road, Hong Kong

Address letters to:
Rangjung Yeshe Publications
P.O. Box 1200,
Kathmandu, Nepal
www.rangjung.com

Fourth edition, revised and expanded, 2009
Printed in the United States of America

Publication Data:
Tsele Natsok Rangdröl
(rtse le rgod tshang pa sna tshogs rang grol, b. 1608).
Full title: *Lamp of Mahamudra, The Immaculate Lamp that Perfectly and Fully
Illuminates the Meaning of Mahamudra, the Essence of all Phenomena.*
Foreword by Dilgo Khyentse Rinpoche.
Introduction by Tulku Urgyen Rinpoche.
Translated from the Tibetan by Erik Pema Kunsang.
Edited by Marcia Binder Schmidt
4th ed.

Tibetan title: *chos thams cad kyi snying po phyag rgya chen poii don yang
dag par rab tu gsal bar byed pa dri ma med paii sgron ma.
The Heart of the Matter: The Unchanging Convergence of Vital
Points that Show Exactly How to Apply the View and Meditation of the
Definitive Meaning (nges don gyi lta sgom nyams su len tshul ji ltar bar
ston pa rdo rjeii mdo ëdzin zhes bya ba bzhugs so).*
Introduction by Chökyi Nyima Rinpoche

ISBN: 978–962–7341–60–4
1. Mahamudra. 2. Vajrayana philosophy—Buddhism.
3. Buddhism—Tibet. I. Title.

Cover design: Marryann Lipaj
Cover photo courtesy of Mani Lama by Tony Hagen 1962

Distributed to the book trade by:
North Atlantic Books & Random House, Inc.
4 5 6 7 8 9 printer 14 13 12 11 10 09

Contents

Contents

The Heart of the Matter

This book is dedicated to the Buddadharma and all sentient beings. It is said that when the teachings of the Buddha flourish, there will be happiness for all beings in this life, in the bardo, and in following lives.

Tulku Urgyen Rinpoche

ADVICE TO MYSELF

Guru, source of refuge, having bowed down at
    your feet,
Today I give myself this piece of pertinent
    advice.

You hypocrite and begging drifter in the darkest
    age.
Many years have passed since through the
    teaching's gate you walked,
But even now your mind has yet to mingle with
    the Dharma.
How shameful is your wallowing in these endless
    strings of thought,
So wouldn't it be better now to blend your mind
    with Dharma?

Young of age you are, but lifespans are uncertain.
Never sure when magic-substance bodies will be
    shed.
Still you're chained by clinging to the pleasures
    of this life,
So wouldn't it be better now to urgently exert
    yourself in Dharma?

Nothing else will help you when you die apart
from Dharma.
But while you have the teachings you still drift
off, so distracted.
How despicable it is just to feign a Dharma
person,
So wouldn't it be better now to achieve the
lasting benefit sublime?

Servant and employees, your enjoyments, goods
and wealth—
You don't see as Dharma-demons of distraction.
Still you yearn to get more worldly fame and
gain,
So wouldn't it be better now to live in solitude
sincerely?

Though you've met a couple of highly qualified
masters,
You have never served them with a genuine
devotion.
How despicable it is just to rival them or
socialize as equals,
So wouldn't it be better now to respect your
samayas?

Without keeping the samayas and vow correctly,
And without being qualified to be a spiritual
guide,
Still you contrive to sit ahead of virtuous people.

So wouldn't it be better now to live alone in
mountain retreats?

Without having solved your general doubts
through learning,
And without having reached the inner
stronghold through meditation,
You still fool yourself with teaching the Dharma
to others.
So wouldn't it be better now to practice the
essential?

You may have received some empowerments and
guiding instructions,
But not really brought them into your stream-
of-being.
How silly it is to live with the Dharma and mind
disconnected.
So wouldn't it be better now to train in the
deepest meaning?

Without having gone through development
stage's approach and accomplishment,
And without possessing the confidence of
completion stage's view,
How deluded it is to pretend to be the refuge of
the dead and the living.
So wouldn't it be better now to seek at least a
refuge for yourself?

Without having matured yourself with the
    ripening empowerments,
And without having soaked yourself with the
    liberating instructions,
Still you fool yourself with pretending to be a
    guide for others.
So wouldn't it be better now to achieve at least
    you own benefit?
So wouldn't it be better now to seek at least a
    refuge for yourself?

When soon you come to the bardo's narrow
    passage
There is indeed help to get from your many
    followers and attendants,
But still you fool yourself with keeping the
    company of Dharmaless people.
So wouldn't it be better now to train alone in
    meditation?

When you lie chained in Yama's demonic chains,
Your wealth cannot help you in the slightest,
But still you fool yourself with hoarding wealth
    and means.
So wouldn't it be better now to reduce this
    craving for material things?

On the border where you chose between samsara
    and nirvana,
To make the untrue choice will bring you lasting
    trouble,

While mundane deeds will all lie wasted and in
vain.
So wouldn't it be better now to find a goal that's
permanent?

Without having cut the concepts of samsaric
things,
And without having aimed your heart at the
Three Jewels,
You will continue to roam repeatedly within
samsara,
So wouldn't it be better now to focus on the
sacred Dharma?

Without understanding that your homeland is a
demon's prison,
And without seeing relatives and friends as
Mara's henchmen,
To cling and remain stuck will just drive you to
the lower realms,
So wouldn't it be better now to cut all likes and
dislikes from their root?

Without remaining at the feet of an authentic
master,
Who will close the doors to rebirth in samsara's
lower realms?
Having given all—your body, life, belongings—
to your guru,
Wouldn't it be better now to seek a refuge with
complete sincerity?

Unless you seek the Dharma and apply the
    practice,
Why would the Dharma ever try to seek you
    out!
Having given yourself, both life and limb, not
    shying away from any troubles,
Wouldn't it be better now to train in the
    profound instructions?

A Dharmaless and indolent man, born in the
    kaliyuga,
Spoke one day these lines of good advice
To give a helpful counsel to himself.
By its merits may all beings quickly reach
    awakening.

Foreword

Kyabje Dilgo Khyentse

The most learned Tsele Pema Lekdrub was the body-emanation of the great translator Vairotsana, and he attained the pinnacle of learning and accomplishment of the masters of the Land of Snow. Also known as Kongpo Götsangpa Natsok Rangdröl, he was unmatched in his three qualities of scholarship, virtue and noble-mindedness.

Among the five volumes of his collected works, I considered that this *Lamp of Mahamudra* would benefit everyone interested in the Dharma. The words are clear and easy to understand, and lengthy scholarly expositions are not emphasized. This text, easy to comprehend and containing all the key points and very direct instructions, results from following the oral advice of a qualified master.

In order to help the foreigners who are presently interested in the Dharma to gain true confidence, I, old Dilgo Khyentse, encouraged my disciple Erik Pema Kunsang to translate this book into English. Therefore, may everyone trust in this.

> *Written on the twenty-fifth day of the first month of the*
> *year of the Earth Dragon by Dilgo Khyentse.*

Summary of Mahamudra

An Introductory Discourse by
Tulku Urgyen Rinpoche

Mahamudra has three modes: Sutra Mahamudra, Mantra Mahamudra, and Essence Mahamudra.

Sutra Mahamudra is attaining the stage of complete buddhahood through traversing the five paths and ten bhumis.

Mantra Mahamudra is experiencing the four joys via the third empowerment, which lead to the four levels of emptiness. The four types: joy, supreme joy, non-joy, and innate joy lead one to the means for realizing the ultimate view of Mahamudra. In the traditional statement "to reach the true wisdom by means of the symbolic wisdom," the symbolic wisdom refers to the four levels of emptiness invoked by the four joys while true wisdom is Mahamudra of the natural state. Introducing Mahamudra of the naked, natural state in this way is called Mantra Mahamudra.

Essence Mahamudra is described in terms of essence, nature, and expression. The essence is nonarising, the nature is unobstructed, and the expression is what manifests in manifold ways. Essence Mahamudra is pointed out through skillful means as follows: "Essence Mahamudra is your naked, ordinary mind resting in unfabricated naturalness."

Although the teachings on Essence Mahamudra and Dzogchen of the Natural State use different terminology, in actuality they do not differ at all. Through such teachings, the mind at the time of death merges with dharmakaya the instant that the material body disintegrates. It is also possible to attain true and complete enlightenment in the dharmadhatu realm of Akanishtha while still remaining in this physical body.

This state of Mahamudra is the flawless realization of all the learned and accomplished masters of India, without exception, the Six Ornaments and Two Supreme Ones as well as the Eighty Mahasiddhas. Simply hearing the word "Mahamudra" leads to the end of samsaric existence.

As Sherab Özer, the great master tertön of Trangpo, wrote:

Mahamudra and the Great Perfection
Differ in words but not in meaning.

In terms of ground, path and fruition, Ground Mahamudra is the nonarising essence, unobstructed nature, and expression manifest in manifold ways. The Dzogchen teachings describe these three aspects as essence, nature and capacity.

Path Mahamudra is naked, ordinary mind left to rest in unfabricated naturalness.

Fruition Mahamudra is the final seizing of the Dharmakaya Throne of Nonmeditation. The Four Yogas of Mahamudra are called One-pointedness, Simplicity, One Taste, and Nonmeditation. The stage of fruition is realized when the dharmakaya throne of nonmeditation is attained.

One-pointedness, the first yoga of Mahamudra, has three levels: lesser, medium, and greater. One-pointedness, for the most part, consists of shamatha and the gradual progression through the stages of shamatha with support, without support, and finally to the shamatha that delights the tathagatas. During this process fixation gradually diminishes.

The next stage, Simplicity, basically means nonfixation. During the three levels of lesser, medium and greater Simplicity, fixation falls more and more apart. While One-pointedness is mainly shamatha, Simplicity emphasizes vipashyana.

One Taste is the state of mind in which shamatha and vipashyana are unified. Appearance and mind arise as one taste. One does not need to confine appearances to being there and consciousness to being here, but the dualistic fixation of appearance and mind mingle into one taste in the space of nonduality.

When in retreat at Gampo Mountain, Lord Gampopa told one of his disciples, "The mingling of appearance and mind is like this!" As he simultaneously moved his hand freely through the room's main pillar, the upper and lower parts of the pillar disconnected, not touching each other. The caretaker was later frightened and thinking the roof would fall down, he placed a piece of slate between the pillar sections. Gampopa's act was an expression of reaching the greater level of One Taste, the stage at which the world and beings, all dualistic phenomena, mingle into one taste in the space of nonduality. Dualistic concepts such as good and bad, pure and impure, pleasure and pain, existence and nonexistence, objects to be accepted or rejected, adopted or avoided, as well as hope and fear: everything intermingles as one taste, the royal seat of dharmakaya.

At this level there still might remain some sense of enjoying the spectacle of one nature, one taste, but at the fourth stage, Nonmeditation, even subtle concepts of watcher and something watched, meditator and object of meditation, are dissolved within the space free from mental constructs. Thus, the Dharmakaya Throne of Nonmeditation is attained. Dzogchen calls this stage the exhaustion of phenomena beyond concepts. Nothing needs to be meditated upon or cultivated; that is dharmakaya.

> At the time of One-pointedness don't fixate.
> During Simplicity don't fall into extremes.
> Don't cling to the taste of One Taste.
> Nonmeditation transcends conceptual mind.

Here I have given a short and comprehensive outline of Mahamudra.

Tulku Urgyen Rinpoche
Nagi Gompa, Nepal 1988.

Lamp of
Mahamudra

PROLOGUE

Namo Mahamudraye.

Perfectly pure since the beginning,
The nature is devoid of all fabricated attributes.
This supreme and lucid wakefulness of dharmata
I worship with the homage of realizing it as it is.

Though no existence is present in the essence
    itself,
Its manifest aspect has the magic of manifold
    appearance.
I shall now explain so you can know your nature,
This natural mode of innate inseparability.

The quintessence of the meaning of all the infinite and countless teachings of the buddhas is that the wisdom essence of the tathagatas is present as the nature of sentient beings. The innumerable different kinds of Dharma teachings and vehicles are indeed only taught for the purpose of realizing this nature. There are as many gates to the Dharma and types of instructions that tame as there are different kinds of inclinations and talents of those to be tamed. This is due to the special and wondrous power of the compassionate activity of all the buddhas.

Among all these different kinds of teachings is one that is the most eminent, the shortest path, the ultimate meaning of the summit of all the vajra vehicles of the resultant Secret Mantra. Renowned like the sun and the moon, Mahamudra is the supreme method that directly and easily reveals the natural face of mind in which the three kayas are spontaneously present. It is the one highway journeyed by all supreme siddhas and vidyadharas. I shall now explain the necessary points of its meaning briefly in three chapters:

1. Ground Mahamudra, the essential nature of things; the meaning of the view, briefly stated in terms of confusion and liberation.
2. Path Mahamudra, the self-existing natural flow; the manner in which the paths and bhumis are traversed, explained extensively in terms of shamatha and vipashyana.
3. Fruition Mahamudra, the manner in which the welfare of beings is accomplished through the realization of the immaculate and ultimate three kayas of buddhahood; explained as the conclusion.

Section One

GROUND MAHAMUDRA

THE VIEW

Ground Mahamudra, the essential nature of things. The meaning of the view briefly stated in terms of confusion and liberation.

Your natural essence cannot be established as either samsara or nirvana. Not confined by any one extreme, free from the limitations of exaggeration and denigration, it is not tainted nor spoiled by such designations as pleasant or unpleasant, being or not being, existent or non-existent, permanent or annihilated, self or other, and so forth. Because it is not established as a certain kind of identity, your essence can serve as the basis for the manifestation of any form or conception to manifest. Yet, no matter how it manifests, ultimately this essence has no true existence. Thus, it is a great emptiness free from the limitations of arising, dwelling and ceasing, the unconditioned dharmadhatu. Since the beginning it is a nature in which the three kayas are spontaneously present and it is known as the "Ground Mahamudra of the essential nature of things." The *Guhyagarbha Tantra* teaches:

This mind-essence devoid of ground and root
Is the basis of all phenomena.

This essence is not something that exists within the mind-stream of just one individual person or just one buddha. It is the actual basis of all that appears and exists, the whole of samsara and nirvana.

When you realize its nature, knowing its real condition, you are called a buddha. When you do not realize it, remaining ignorant of it and experiencing confusion, you are called a sentient being. Thus it serves as the basis for wandering in samsara and is known as the general ground of samsara and nirvana. Saraha, the Great Brahmin, stated:

This single mind, the seed of everything,
From it manifest samsara and nirvana.

It is a single essence with different manifestations, or with different aspects appearing, simply due to the difference between having or not having realized it. Whichever of either of these two occurs, it still abides as the great primordial indivisibility of the three kayas with neither good or bad nor any defect such as changeability tainting its essence. The general vehicles call this the "unchanging absolute." It is also the primordial ground nature.

This nature present as a neutral and undetermined ground neither realized nor not realized, is known as "all-ground," "alaya," because it forms the basis for both

samsara and nirvana. This all-ground, not a mere nihilistic and void nothingness, is self-luminous knowing that
occurs unceasingly. That knowing, called "all-ground
consciousness," is like a mirror and its brightness.

The Basic Split

Now follows an explanation of how the split between
samsara and nirvana arose from this single all-ground.

As for the knowing quality or wisdom aspect of this
self-luminous consciousness, its essence is empty, its
nature is knowing and these two are indivisible as the
core of awareness. Being the seed or cause of all the buddha qualities and attributes of the pure paths, this is also
known as the "true all-ground of application," "sugata-
essence," "dharmakaya of self-knowing," "transcendent
knowledge," "buddha of your own mind," and so forth.
All these names given to the classifications of nirvanic
attributes are synonymous. This wisdom aspect is exactly
what should be realized and recognized by everyone who
has entered the path.

Due to the ignorant aspect of this neutral all-ground,
you do not know your own essence and the natural state
is not realized. In this way you have obscured yourself.
Called "coemergent ignorance" or the "great darkness of
beginningless time," since it is the basis from which all
disturbing emotions and deluded thoughts arise it is also
known as the "all-ground of various tendencies." Hence

it is the ground of confusion of all sentient beings. The *Tantra of Directly Realizing* explains:

> Since awareness did not arise from the ground,
> This completely mindless oblivion
> Is the very cause of ignorance and confusion.

Accompanying this ignorance are also the seven thought states resulting from delusion, such as medium clinging and forgetfulness.

From this coemergent ignorance arises a fixation on an ego and self-entity. On the basis of this "self" arises the fixation on "other." Not recognizing this personal manifestation for what it is, a personal manifestation, one grasps at it as though it were an external object. This onset of confusion through not recognizing the nature of the thoughts of fixation on perceiver and perceived is called "conceptual ignorance" or "mind consciousness." It is the cognitive act of confusing object and mind as being separate and is accompanied by the forty thought states resulting from desire, such as attachment and clinging.

From the expression of this mind consciousness, various kinds of tendencies and confusions will arise and unfold. Aiding that, through the power of the solidifying force of dependent origination, such as the condition of the all-pervasive wind of karma and the cause of the ignorant aspect of the all-ground, the body, appearances and mind are fully formed. The different sense consciousnesses of the five sense-doors and the manifestation of perceptions and thoughts of the six collections are also called the "dependent."

The five major root winds and the five minor branch winds provide the vehicle for the thoughts. Through the power of being habituated to confused fixation, your personal manifestations will appear as a world with inhabitants. Based on this foundation and objects, everything is produced. Also known as the "defiled mind," it is what moves through the different five sense-doors, creating attachment and so forth. Therefore it is also called the "consciousnesses of the five senses." Accompanying it are also the thirty-three thought states resulting from anger, such as medium detachment and so forth.

In that way, the all-ground of various tendencies as the root and the eighty innate thought states as the branches gradually grow and confusion becomes continuous. Through this you wander endlessly in samsara. That is the way of confusion of unrealized sentient beings.

Because of that confusion, the tendencies for all the phenomena of samsara and nirvana remain in this all-ground in the manner of seeds. The various objects of gross materiality and the pure and impure parts of channel, wind and essence of the inner body as well as all the various external phenomena of samsara and nirvana, the worlds and beings of the three realms, appear externally in an interdependent manner. All of these, however, like objects appearing in a dream are a magical display of superficial appearances which do not actually exist. Growing more and more used to fixating on them as being permanent, solidifying and clinging to them as being real, you experience the various kinds of pleasure, pain, and indifference of the three realms and six classes of beings. You spin perpetually through the causes and effects of samsara as though on the rim of a water wheel. The general characteristics of sentient beings are indeed like this.

How the Essence Remains

Although confused in this way and wandering in samsara, the nature of the sugata-essence, your essence of awareness, has become neither impaired nor decreased even in the slightest. The *Tantra of the Two Segments* says:

> Every being is a buddha,
> But obscured by passing veils.

In the ultimate sense, this primordial nature is vividly present as the inseparable three kayas. Moreover, even when obscured by the passing stains of deluded experience, this natural face of the essence is still vividly present as the three kayas. Finally, it is also vividly present as the three kayas at the time of realizing the fruition, when what obscures has been cleared away and when the two-fold knowledge is perfected. For this reason, the duality of confusion and liberation is simply a label given to the mere state of not being free from the stains of deluded thinking and ignorance. The *Uttaratantra* declares:

As before, it is so after;
It is a changeless nature.

Although the nature of mind is spontaneously perfect as the primordially pure essence, this temporary confusion or coemergent ignorance through which you have obscured yourself originated from yourself, like an impurity covering gold. Various means of purifying and cleansing these obscurations have been taught. This essence, which itself is self-existing wakefulness, unchanging throughout the three times and devoid of conceptual constructs, is the actual knowledge aspect. All the paths can therefore be included under "means and knowledge." That is the ultimate realization of the victorious ones.

You might think, "Isn't it illogical that the single all-ground explained above should split into both samsara and nirvana?" In fact, it resembles the medicine camphor, which causes either benefit or harm depending on whether a sickness stems from heat or cold. Moreover, a single poisonous substance that will normally cause death can become medicine if utilized by some skillful means such as a mantra. Similarly, you are liberated when you are aware of and recognize the single nature of the all-ground and deluded when ignorant of the all-ground and apprehending it as a self-entity. Thus, the all-ground is only changed by realizing or not realizing. Noble Nagarjuna has taught:

One is called a "sentient being"
While veiled by webs of negative emotion.

One is called "buddha"
When freed from these emotions.

For this reason, embracing all phenomena with the skillful means of the Mahamudra instructions of the essential true meaning, you will attain innate stability in the nature of ground Mahamudra. You will purify the impurities of confused thought by path Mahamudra and capture the royal throne of the three kayas, which is fruition Mahamudra. Thus, you will open up for the treasure of the twofold benefit. A karmically destined person who is a worthy recipient should therefore search for a truly qualified master endowed with the nectar of blessings and follow him according to the example of how Sadaprarudita followed Manibhadra or how Naropa followed Tilopa. You should definitely have your being ripened by either extensive or condensed procedures of ripening empowerments, the main entrance door to the path of Vajrayana. Then you should exert yourself in each and every one of the general and special preliminaries until some signs manifest, without giving in to comfort-seeking, indolence or belittling the practice. This is to be highly treasured as the beginning guidance of the liberating instructions.

In particular, through the richness of devotion to your master, you should emphasize practicing without hypocrisy. Furthermore, you should be sure to receive the warmth of his blessings. This is the sacred essence of the tradition of all accomplished Kagyu vidyadharas. The *Great Pacifying River Tantra* declares:

This coemergent wakefulness, beyond
    description,
Is recognized only through the practices of
    gathering accumulations and purifying one's
    veils
And through the blessings of a realized master.
Know it to be delusion if you depend on other
    means.

Now comes the main part itself. No matter which style of teaching one follows according to the traditions of practice of the different lineages—recognizing the meditation from within the view or establishing the view from within the meditation—the exclusively important chief point is to receive the blessings of the lineage masters.

The Actual View

In general, the different vehicles and the various philosophical schools have countless ways of accepting a view and each in essence has a true, established basis. Since all the vehicles are the infinite display of the all-encompassing modes of activity of the victorious ones, I will not describe them with such words as pure or impure, good or bad, but only rejoice in them.

In this context, the view is the mind-essence—spontaneously present since the beginning as the great and total purity. Free throughout the three times of past, present, and future from the constructs of arising, dwelling, and ceasing as well as of coming and going, this mind-essence is unspoiled by the conceptual attributes of fixating on samsara, nirvana, and the path. It is not exaggerated or denigrated as existence or nonexistence, being or not being, permanence or annihilation, good or bad, high or low. It transcends refutation and proof, accepting and rejecting, changing and altering any of all the appearing and existing phenomena that comprise samsara and nirvana.

The exact nature of this original state or mode of being is totally free in being inseparable appearance and emptiness and vividly clear in being the unity of wakefulness and emptiness. It is utterly open in being all-pervasive primordial freedom and completely even in being unconditioned spontaneous presence. This is the main body of the view, the natural state as it is, primordially self-existing and originally present as the essence of all of samsara and nirvana. There is no other separate piece or fragment of a view than this.

To see the inherent falsity in dualistic fixation through understanding this primordial condition is called "realizing the view," and also "seeing the mind-essence" or "knowing the nature of things." As described in the *Dohakosha:*

When realized, everything is that.
No one can realize anything superior.

In actuality, all of appearance and existence, samsara and nirvana, is the display of the three kayas. Your own mind as well has the nature of the three kayas and itself is not apart from ultimate dharmadhatu. All samsaric attributes are contained within the mode of the mind's characteristics. All attributes of the path are contained within the mode of the Dharma. All attributes of fruition are contained within the mode of the mind's capability.

The nonarising essence of the mind itself is dharmakaya, its unobstructed nature is sambhogakaya and its expression manifesting in any way whatsoever is nirmanakaya. These three kayas are again spontaneously present as an indivisible identity. To recognize and settle on this natural state is called perfectly realizing the faultless and correct view. A view different from this—a view or meditation imputed through intellectual concepts of assumption or through attributes of reference such as being free or not free from extremes, high or special, good or bad and so forth—has never been taught as the view of Mahamudra.

Section Two

PATH MAHAMUDRA

SHAMATHA AND VIPASHYANA

**The meditation of path Mahamudra.
Explaining shamatha and vipashyana,
faults and virtues, meditation and
post-meditation, misunderstandings,
how to traverse the path, and so forth.**

The term "meditation" and the ways of meditating in the contexts of each of the numberless philosophical schools generally have numerous meanings; but here, the word "meditation" is merely given to the act of acquainting mind with the meaning of the natural state, the view as explained above. You never meditate by fabricating something mentally such as a concrete object with color and shape. Nor should you deliberately meditate while suppressing the mind's thinking or perceptions, as in meditation on a constructed emptiness. Meditation means simply sustaining the naturalness of your mind without any fabrication.

In particular, there are various kinds of mental capacities and intelligence. People with sharp faculties, the instantaneous type who are realized through former training, can possibly be liberated simultaneously with recognizing their essence, with no need to be guided gradually through shamatha and vipashyana. But, other ordinary types of people must be guided gradually. Therefore, begin with training yourself in the stages of shamatha with attributes, by focusing on a stick, stone, deity image, or syllable; or train in the practices of wind and essence and so forth. Having attained confidence in these practices, then engage in the supreme shamatha without attributes.

Shamatha

The actual shamatha is taught through the following three meditation techniques:

1. Not letting the mind wander after any outer or inner object, rest in undistracted freshness.
2. Not controlling your three doors by being too tight, rest freely in effortless naturalness.
3. Not letting the essence of a thought and the wakefulness be separate and different as if applying an antidote, rest in the natural clarity of self-aware self-knowing.

Other names, such as "nondistraction," "nonmeditation," and "nonfabrication," are also used for these three.

The three gates of emancipation taught in the general vehicles are contained within these three as well: The mind itself refraining from following after one's actions or what happened concerning past actions and events is called the "emancipation-gate of marklessness." Your present mind, free from mind-made tampering and construction or the negating and affirming acts of "Now this appears! This is what I should do!" is itself the "emancipation-gate of emptiness." Being free from anticipating that such and such is to occur in the future as well as being free from desire and yearning, such as hoping that meditation will happen or fearing that it will not, is the emancipation-gate of wishlessness. These are, in short, included within simply letting your mind rest in naturalness—unspoiled and without fabrication.

When a thought suddenly manifests in that state, simply vividly recognizing your essence without following after what occurred is sufficient. Do not try deliberately to inhibit it, to concentrate inwardly in meditation or to control it with some other remedy. Whatever action of that type you might take is not the vital point of sustaining the mind-nature in uncontrived nonfabrication.

Although other paths contain various teachings about this, the context here has only the path of recognizing the essence of whatever occurs; if you search for some other technique it will not be the meditation of Mahamudra. As the Great Brahmin declared:

> Effort spoils a person's meditation training.
> While there is not a "thing" in which to train,
> Don't be distracted, even for an instant.
> This, I say, is Mahamudra meditation.

By thus resting evenly in the nature of mind as it is, the three experiences of shamatha will gradually manifest. What are they? At first, the mind seems more agitated, with even more thought activity than before. Sometimes between thought activity, your mind remains still for a short while. Do not regard such thought activity as a defect. Although up to now your mind has been always thinking, you did not recognize that. This point, of recognizing the difference between thinking and stillness, is the first shamatha experience, like the waterfall on a mountain cliff.

After maintaining the practice like that, the thoughts will be mostly controlled. You become gentle and relaxed; both your body and mind become totally blissful and you do not feel like engaging in other activities, but only delight in meditation. Except on rare occasions, you remain mostly free from any thought activity. That is the intermediate shamatha stage, like the gentle flow of a river.

Later on, after practicing with undistracted endeavor, your body becomes totally blissful, free from any painful sensation. Your mind is clear knowing free from thoughts. Not noticing the passing of day and night, you can remain unmoved for as long as you are resting in meditation and you are unharmed by faults. The manifest disturbing emotions have subsided and you have no strong clinging to such things as food and clothing. You have conditioned superknowledges, and various kinds of visionary experiences occur. The manifestation of these numerous kinds of ordinary qualities is the final state of shamatha which is like an unmoving ocean.

Many meditators who at this point do not connect with an experienced master and who have great diligence but little learning, become infatuated with these seemingly good qualities. Also, ordinary people see them as siddhas and that leads to the danger of creating disaster for both self and others. So be careful.

This endeavor in shamatha meditation does not qualify as the main part of Mahamudra practice, but it is certainly essential as a foundation. Gyalwa Lorey has said:

> Dull shamatha without clarity,
> You may meditate on for a long time without
> realizing the nature.
> Possessing the gaze with sharp awareness,
> Meditate by continuing short sessions.

The Vipashyana of the Main Part

Without completely clarifying doubts about resolving whether or not the nature of your mind has any concrete attributes, such as shape or color and so forth, whether it has a place of origin, dwelling and departure, whether it arises and ceases, whether it is existent or nonexistent, permanent or annihilated, or whether it has a center and a limit, you will be unable to arrive at the view as it truly is. Lacking that, you will not know how to sustain the meditation naturally and spontaneously. Not knowing that, regardless how much deluded shamatha and persevering mind-fixing you may do, you will not transcend the cause and effect of the three realms of samsara. You should therefore clear away your misconceptions in the presence of a qualified master.

In particular, the Secret Mantra being the path of blessings, you should exert yourself in devotion and supplication the means for assimilating the realization of the lineage masters' blessings. By doing that, you will directly experience your own awareness which, as explained above in the context of the view, is spontaneously present since the very beginning as the essence of the dharmakaya. You will experience it as a direct and nonconceptual wakefulness, which does not fall into any of the extremes of existence or nonexistence, eternalism or nihilism. Although experienced and understood as being cognizant, aware, empty, and indivisible, this wakefulness cannot be illustrated by analogies and it transcends any means of expression through words. This state of being—wide awake in self-existing and natural knowing—is indeed what is called vipashyana.

First of all, ordinary people have never, for even a single instant, been separate from this natural knowing. Yet, because of not having embraced it with oral instructions or blessings they haven't recognized it. Next, this natural knowing is what remains in shamatha and what observes whether or not there is stillness or thinking. It is the doer of all these things. Yet, it is like not seeing yourself. The projection of a train of thought by an ordinary person is nothing other than vipashyana itself manifesting as conceptual thinking. Moreover, the experiences of shamatha as well as bliss, clarity, and nonthought are nothing other than the vipashyana awareness manifesting as such experiences. But because of not recognizing your naked essence free from concepts these experiences have become a mere sustaining of stillness and not the cause for enlightenment. After you have recognized your own essence, there is not a single state, be it stillness or thinking, which is not vipashyana or Mahamudra. Lorepa clarified this:

> When you are not involved in mental fixation,
> Whatever manifests as the objects of the six
>   collections,
> Everything is self-liberated personal experience.
> Have you realized this inseparability, you
>   meditators?

The Unity of Shamatha and Vipashyana

Shamatha is generally held to mean abiding in the state of bliss, clarity and nonthought after conceptual thinking has naturally subsided. Vipashyana means to see nakedly and vividly the essence of mind which is self-knowing, objectless and free from exaggeration and denigration. In another way, shamatha is said to be the absence of thought activity and vipashyana is recognizing the essence of thought. Numerous other such statements exist but, in actuality, whatever manifests or is experienced does not transcend the inseparability of shamatha and vipashyana. Stillness and thinking both are nothing but the display of the mind alone; to recognize your essence at the time of either stillness or thinking is itself the nature of vipashyana.

Shamatha is not to become involved in solidified clinging to any of the external appearances of the six collections, while vipashyana is the unobstructed manifestation of perception. Thus within perception the unity of shamatha and vipashyana is complete.

Vividly recognizing the essence of the thought as it suddenly occurs is shamatha. Directly liberating it within natural mind, free from concepts, is vipashyana. Thus within conceptual thinking shamatha and vipashyana are also a unity.

Furthermore, looking into the essence without solidly following after a disturbing emotion even when it arises intensely is shamatha. The empty and naked knowing within which the observing awareness and the observed disturbing emotion have no separate existence is vipashyana. Thus the unity of shamatha and vipashyana is complete within disturbing emotions as well.

Summary

The essence of your own mind does not exist as stillness or thinking, projection or dissolution, good or bad. All phenomena that appear are merely the unobstructed manifestation, the display of your mind. Similarly, shamatha and vipashyana themselves have no existence other than as an indivisible unity. However, so that people can easily understand, their manifestation has been taught under different names and classifications.

Shamatha alone has therefore been stated to be ineffective as the main part of Mahamudra meditation because:

Stillness alone is the mundane dhyana.

The dhyanas of the non-Buddhist extremists and even the Buddhist dhyanas of the shravakas and pratyekabuddhas as well as the samadhis of all the god realms are ordinary. They are therefore not the actual path of the fourth empowerment of Mantra. In particular, in Mahamudra clinging to the experience of stillness is inadmissible. Mahamudra is the occasion for practicing what appears and exists as being dharmakaya. If one accepts stillness as good, as being meditation, and rejects thinking as bad, as not being meditation, that does not accord with appearance and existence being dharmakaya, or with whatever arises being Mahamudra, or with leaving whatever occurs free from fabrication.

Faults and Qualities

Having briefly discussed the meaning of shamatha and vipashyana, I shall now explain something about faults and qualities as well as the different kinds of error.

The two parts are: In general, the explanation of the mistake of not understanding how to sustain resting in equanimity; and in particular, the explanation of how to clear away the faults of the different types of errors and deviations.

Explanation of Mistakes

Resting one's mind without fabrication is considered the single key point of the realization of all the countless profound and extensive oral instructions in meditation practice such as Mahamudra, Dzogchen, Lamdrey, Chö, Zhije and so forth. The oral instructions appear in various modes due to the difference in ways of human understanding.

Some meditators regard meditation practice as simply a thought-free state of mind in which all gross and subtle perceptions of the six senses have ceased. That is called straying into a dull state of shamatha.

Some presume stable meditation to be a state of neutral dullness not embraced by mindfulness.

Some regarding meditation as complete clarity, smooth bliss or utter voidness and cling to those experiences.

Some chop their meditation into fragments, believing the objective of meditation to be a vacant state of mind between the cessation of one thought and the arising of the next.

Some hold on to such thoughts as, "The mind-nature is dharmakaya! It is empty! It cannot be grasped!" To think, "Everything is devoid of true existence! It is like a magical illusion! It is like space!" and to regard that as the meditation state is to have fallen into the extreme of intellectual assumption.

Some people claim that whatever is thought or whatever occurs is of the nature of meditation. They stray into craziness by falling under the power of ordinary thinking.

Most others regard thinking as a defect and inhibit it. They believe in resting in meditation after controlling what is being thought and tie themselves up in fixated mindfulness or an ascetic state of mind.

In short, the mind may be still, in turmoil as thoughts and disturbing emotions, or tranquil in any of the experiences of bliss, clarity, and nonthought. Knowing how to sustain the spontaneity of innate naturalness directly in whatever occurs, without having to fabricate, reject or change anything is extremely rare. It seems necessary to have a faultless practice in harmony with the actual statements of realization in such texts as the sutras and tantras of definitive meaning as well as the collected works, oral instructions and guidance manuals of the lineage of accomplished masters.

Clearing Away Specific Errors and Mistakes

All the forefathers of the Practice Lineage having taught this in detail and extensively, I shall here explain the errors simply, as a brief indication.

Clinging to any of the three experiences of bliss, clarity, or nonthought while resting in meditation will create the causes for rebirth in the three realms of Desire, Form and Formlessness. Being reborn there, you will, when your life span ends, again fall down into the lower realms. Thus, they are not the path to buddhahood.

Dividing up this topic in detail, there are in particular the nine dhyanas of absorption. When resting evenly in shamatha, then, to be free from gross thoughts of perceiver and perceived, but still to be fettered by the concept of meditator and meditation object is called the "samadhi of the First Dhyana." Why is that? Because this is what is being meditated upon in all the abodes of the gods of the First Dhyana. Meditating in this way creates the cause for being reborn there as a god at the level of the First Dhyana.

Likewise, the second dhyana is to be free from the state of mind of concept and discernment, but still to experience the taste of the samadhi of joy and bliss.

The third dhyana is to be free from mental movement, but supported merely by the inhalation and exhalation of breath.

The fourth dhyana is to be free from all kinds of thoughts, a state of samadhi which is unobstructed clarity, like space.

Supreme among all the mundane samadhis, these are the foundation for vipashyana. If meditated upon with attachment, however, they become a deviation from Mahamudra causing rebirth as gods in the abodes of those dhyanas.

Furthermore, thinking "All phenomena are infinite like space!" or "This consciousness, free from partiality and nonexistent, is infinite!" or "Perception, being neither existent nor nonexistent, is not an action of mind!" or "This mind is voidness, which is nothing whatsoever!"— Dwelling in the states of these four levels has the defect of straying into the four formless spheres of finality; called the Infinite Space, Infinite Consciousness, Neither Presence nor Absence, and Nothing Whatsoever.

The shravaka's samadhi of peace is the state of mind that has abandoned these four thoughts in which involvement in objects has been blocked, and in which you abide having interrupted the movements of the wind-mind. Although such a state is taught to be the ultimate shamatha, in this context it is not a faultless meditation unless embraced by vipashyana.

Each of these nine dhyanas of absorption has some temporary qualities, such as accomplishment of superknowledges and miraculous powers. Here, however, you should attain the ultimate result of complete enlightenment and not merely relative or superficial qualities. Thus, if these are accomplished naturally and you then cling to them or feel arrogant, know that to be a direct obstacle for enlightenment.

The Eight Deviations

Having explained these errors and ways of going astray, I shall now teach the eight deviations:

1. Not understanding that the mind-essence is the unity of appearance and emptiness endowed with the supreme of all aspects, the unobstructed interdependence of cause and effect, you slip into focusing on the empty aspect. Acknowledge this fault called "basic straying from the essence of emptiness."

2. Similarly, after engaging in meditation, although you may have merely intellectually understood the meaning of the natural state, experience has not arisen in yourself. Or, again forgetting that which has arisen, the meaning will not be present within your being although you might be able to explain the words to others. That is called "temporary straying from the essence."

3. While what is needed at present is the path itself, you desire to attain some other result later on. That is called "basic straying from the path."

4. To regard the sustaining of the ordinary wakefulness of your mind as insufficient while you desire a magnificent mind-made meditation and then search for it elsewhere is called "temporary straying from the path."

5. When something such as a disturbing emotion arises, not to know how to take its essence as the path and instead to meditate on some other technique according to the lower vehicles is called "basic straying from the remedy."

6. Not knowing how to take whatever arises, such as a thought, as the path, but to block off that instance or having to destroy it before resting in meditation is called "deviation into the temporary straying from the remedy."

7. Not understanding that the natural state of the mind essence is primordially empty and rootless, and fabricating such thoughts as "It does not possess a self-nature!" or "It is emptiness!" or "It is just temporarily empty!" is called "basic straying into generalized emptiness."

8. Thinking, "Formerly I was distracted following after thoughts, but now I am meditating nicely!" and then remaining in the state of perpetuating that thought, or, thinking that you have mindfulness when you do not and so forth is called "temporary straying into generalizing."

Summary

Not recognizing the key point of the natural state and not resolving doubts about how it actually is, you risk straying into these and various other kinds of incorrect, look-alike meditations. Exertion in an incorrect, look-alike meditation, for no matter how long is fruitless. Some people create the causes and conditions for an evil state, such as being reborn as a naga by meditating on shamatha cessation. You must therefore have an unmistaken meditation.

Moreover, some people regard a dull or sluggish state of mind free from thoughts as shamatha. They presume that vipashyana means analyzing with thoughts. They believe that a solid and rigid fixing of the mind is mindfulness and mistake a state of neutral indifference for the natural. They confuse the ordinary mind of a commoner, who has not seen the original face of the natural state, for the innate ordinary mind free from fabrication. They regard the clinging to a good samadhi or the mere conditioned bliss of being free from pain as the innate supreme bliss. They mistake the involvement in clinging to apparent objects without having attained the certainty of recognizing the objectless natural state for the unobstructed self-knowing that is free from object and fixation. They confuse the stupidity in which knowing is blocked for being nonconceptual wakefulness and so forth.

In short, all the different types of mistakes, incorrect look-alikes, strayings and deviations, are primarily caused by not having applied oneself fully to the key points of the preliminaries, such as gathering the accumulations and purifying the obscurations. Hence, the defilements of negative karma have not been cleared away. Next, not having treated yourself with the ointment of blessings, your mind is uncured and inflexible. Not having resolved your doubts in the main part of the practice, you have become insensitively caught up in theory and absorbed in words. Finally, not having taken the practice to heart, you have become a person with a dharmic exterior who is neither a practitioner nor a lay person and who ruins the teachings of the Practice Lineage. There are many of that kind in this final end of the dark age. The *Sutra of the Ten Wheels of Kshitigarbha* states:

> Not accepting the cause and effect of the
>   ripening of karma,
> One is a non-Buddhist proponent of nihilism
> And is reborn in the Avichi hell right after dying.
> It will ruin others and destroy oneself.

You must therefore exert yourself intelligently and not become like that.

EXPERIENCE AND
REALIZATION

Endeavor one-pointedly to rest in equanimity without falling prey to mistaken or deluded views and meditations and without going astray or deviating. Also, embrace the ensuing understanding with mindfulness without remaining in the confused dissipation of ordinary abandonment. You will then have some experience and realization in accordance with the particular type of person you are or your degree of mental capacity.

In general, due to the many different systems of the various learned and accomplished masters numerous different ways of identifying these experiences and realizations have appeared. Some say that among the four yogas, after reaching Simplicity, there is no actually outlined meditation and postmeditation. Some make the division into a different meditation and postmeditation for each experience and realization respectively. Some teach a different meditation and postmeditation for each of the individual stages of the four yogas. Innumerable different ways indeed exist.

Similarly, there are various systems concerning the differences between experience and realization. Some have taught that the three levels of One-pointedness are only experience and not actual realization. The different teachings appear to have countless details, such as accepting that the mind-essence is seen at the time of having reached Nonmeditation and so forth.

Since all these teachings are compassionate manifestations intended as means to tame the infinite number of inclinations and dispositions of people, respectfully speaking, you need not regard one teaching as the exclusive truth. I, myself, have not reached, perceived or understood all these stages. So how can I set down any maxims as to what is the case and reasonable or that such and such is not the case and unreasonable? That would be like a person born blind who cannot distinguish between beautiful and ugly colors. Based on my own degree of understanding however, I shall now describe these stages in brief.

Meditation and Postmeditation

The terms and examples for meditation and post-meditation are present during all cultivations of the two stages. The two stages of Vajrayana practice are development stage and completion stage. How is that? The word "meditation" means to focus on the actual thing to be practiced without mixing it with other activities, and the word "postmeditation" means mingling it with other activities, such as during practice breaks. The state of mind at that time is called "ensuing understanding" and perceptions termed "ensuing perception." In general all systems designate them like this. Also, in this context, one can call it "meditation" when beginners are exerting themselves in the actual meditation practice and "post-meditation" when they are doing things such as walking, moving about, eating, sleeping and so forth. For the eminent practitioners, meditation and postmeditation are inseparable; always free from distraction and confusion, their practice is continuous.

Experience and Realization

As for the distinction between experience and realization, "experience" refers to a certain virtuous practice of any high or low level which is not mingled with the essence of mind and which includes something to be relinquished and its remedy. Or one can say that experience is to retain the concept of a separate meditator and meditation object. "Realization" means that the virtuous practice and mind are not separate, but manifest as the essence of mind which is resolved in the attainment of certainty. In short, these two aspects appear not only in the context of actual meditation but also refer to most of the practices of the path such as guru yoga, compassion and bodhichitta, development stage and so forth.

The following example describes this. Having heard from others a rough idea or the story about the Vajra Throne, when its shape and scenery appear in your mind and you can explain it to others, this is called "intellectual understanding." Approaching Vajra Throne from a distance or looking at a drawing of its architectural outlines so that your mind comprehends its approximate meaning, is called "experience." Having gone to Vajra Throne yourself, looked at it carefully and felt certain about it is called the arising of "realization."

Three Types of People

Whether or not these points are easily comprehended depends upon the mental capacities of individual people. These can be divided into three degrees. People who give rise to understanding, experience and realization by merely being shown a symbol or who, in one instant quickly perfect the qualities without having to exert themselves through hardship are called the "instantaneous type." These are great beings who have realization through former training. People whose qualities of experience and realization increase and decrease without sequential order or without being fixed as high or low are called the "skipping the grades type," those with middling capacity. Other general or ordinary people of the type who ascends in definite progressive stages, according to their degree of diligence, are called the "gradual type," which includes all ordinary people. Since the former two can also be included within the progressive stages of the path conforming to the gradual type, I shall here explain according to the gradual way.

THE FOUR YOGAS

The common vehicles teach that one journeys to buddhahood through the ten bhumis and five paths. But here I shall explain the four gradual stages of yoga particularly famed among the lineage masters of the incomparable Dakpo Kagyu. These four yogas, each divided into lesser, medium and higher stages, resulting in twelve, are the meaning nature of the scripture called the *Tantra of the Inconceivable Secret*, elucidated by Lord Dawö Shönnu. That tantra teaches:

> By the samadhi of the Majestic Lion,
> Your clear mind of immovable One-pointedness
>   is radiant.
> It awakens self-knowing wakefulness from
>   within,
> And with stable Acceptance you abandon the
>   suffering of the lower realms.
>
> By the second, the samadhi of Magical Illusion,
> Out of the great meditation of Simplicity,
> Appears the inconceivable as the power of
>   samadhi.
> And having attained the Heat, you gain mastery
>   over rebirth.

By the third, the samadhi of Courageous
    Movement,
Multiplicity being One Taste, the realization of
    the ten bhumis manifests.
You accomplish the benefit of others as a son of
    the jinas of the three times,
And having attained the Summit, your progress
    in uninterrupted.

By the fourth, the Vajralike samadhi,
Out of endeavoring in the practice of
    Nonmeditation,
Your wisdom knowledge perceives the buddha
    realms.
Effortlessly and spontaneously present, it is the
    great state of the Supreme Attribute.

These stages and their corresponding meaning are extensively described in the *Lankavatara Sutra* as well. Acharya Shantipa likewise has elucidated this in great detail through explaining the five eyes, omniscience, and so forth. Moreover, according to the Mahamudra system of the Nyingma tradition, Guru Rinpoche has also taught their meaning concisely. In the *Notes on Vital Points* he describes One-pointedness:

With virtue and evil purified in the mind
You automatically relinquish unvirtuous actions.

Simplicity:

> With mind-essence free from mental constructs
> You relinquish all fixations of perceiver and
>   perceived.

One Taste:

> With appearances arising as dharmakaya
> You automatically relinquish conceptual
>   thinking.

And Nonmeditation:

> By recognizing samsara and nirvana to be devoid
>   of self-nature
> You relinquish all dualistic fixations.

Thus, he taught the four yogas combined with the four exertions. Furthermore, Guru Rinpoche taught:

> Heat is to see the nature of mind.
> By Summit you realize nonarising as
>   dharmakaya.
> Through Acceptance you transcend rejecting
>   samsara and adopting nirvana.
> Supreme Attribute is samsara and nirvana
>   dissolving into mind.

This teaching combines the four yogas with the four aspects of ascertainments on the path of joining, the meaning of which corresponds with the above.

The Four Yogas

As just a humble indication, I shall now explain the progressive way in which the actual meaning of these four yogas manifests and in addition how the ten bhumis and the five paths of the Sutra system are perfected.

Among One-pointedness, Simplicity, One Taste, and Nonmeditation, first is the yoga of One-pointedness:

One pointedness

When a worthy person who has cut attachment to this life and perceives his master as a buddha in person, has received genuine blessings and then rests in evenness, he abides in the states of bliss, clarity and nonthought and acquires certainty. To retain the fixation of thinking, "Meditation is the self-liberation of arising thoughts through recognition" is the lesser One-pointedness.

Although the forefathers of the Practice Lineage regarded the three stages of One-pointedness as only shamatha, according to my own understanding there must of course be different levels of people. Furthermore, for someone who has recognized the innate state, the nature of things is that shamatha and vipashyana are always present as a unity. Therefore, understand that here shamatha is embraced by vipashyana. The ensuing understanding at this point is dominated by fixation on solidity, and during the dream state you are also not much different from an ordinary person. In short, since at this time you are a beginner, you have various kinds of highs and lows in the ease or difficulty of maintaining the practice.

At the time of the medium One-pointedness, you can remain in the meditation state for as long as you desire. At times, samadhi occurs even without having meditated. The ensuing understanding grows less fixated on solidity so that perceptions become wide open and virtuous practice sometimes occurs during sleep as well. It is, in short, the time of meditation becoming meditation.

Following that comes the greater One-pointedness. Throughout day and night, the meditation state becomes, an uninterrupted experience of bliss, clarity and non-thought. Without divisions into ensuing experience, ensuing understanding and so forth, your samadhi becomes continuous. You are free from outer or inner parasites and do not become involved in clinging to sense pleasures. It is taught that you will also attain some superknowledges and miraculous powers. Up to this point, however, you are not free from the experiences of clinging to something excellent and are not liberated from the fetter of conceptual mind fixating on meditation.

Numerous differences exist in levels of capacity of those who have begun these three stages of One-pointedness as well as in the individual degree of their diligence. That is to say, whether or not you have seen the essence of One-pointedness is said to depend upon whether or not you have attained the confidence of self-knowing within the states of bliss, clarity and nonthought. Likewise, the difference between whether or not you have perfected the training lies in the difference between these experiences being continuous or occasional. Whether or not thought arises as meditation depends upon whether or not all arising thoughts become meditation by merely being embraced by mindfulness. Moreover, the arising of qualities depends upon whether or not your mind-stream has become pliable. The sowing of the seed of the rupakaya depends upon whether or not unfabricated compassion arises during the ensuing understanding. The difference between mastering and not mastering the relative lies in whether or not you have achieved certainty in the dependent connection of cause and effect. There are the measurements taught by the Kagyu forefathers.

Simplicity

Having given rise to some extent to these experiences of One-pointedness, if you exert yourself in supplication and practice, without falling prey to the faults of self-centered arrogance or clinging to something excellent, you will ascend to Simplicity. In other words, you will realize correctly that the natural state of your mind-essence is free from the extremes of arising, dwelling and ceasing. During the ensuing understanding, you are liberated when, having embraced that state with mindfulness, it turns into the state of meditation. However, if not embraced with mindfulness, your postmeditation state becomes fixation on solidity. During dreams it is also uncertain whether or not you are confused. In any case, the lesser Simplicity is when you retain some fixation on emptiness, such as thinking, "All phenomena of appearance and existence are nothing but emptiness!"

At the time of the medium Simplicity, this fixation on emptiness and the clinging to the nature of thoughts as being real have been purified. Your clinging to outer appearances as being real, however, is not completely eliminated. During the ensuing understanding and during sleep, deluded fixation and clinging to solidity alternate between being present and absent and you undergo numerous fluctuations in your spiritual practice as well.

The greater Simplicity is having completely cut misconceptions about samsara and nirvana, outer and inner, appearance and mind, and so forth. Thus, you are liberated from clinging to "perceived" or "not perceived," "empty" or "not empty," and so forth. Daytime meditation is for the most part uninterrupted, while deluded fixation sometimes occurs during dreams. However, mindfulness has not yet become continuous, so a slightly deliberate mindfulness is necessary. In short, during these stages of Simplicity, because you mainly experience emptiness and have the experience of not fixating on anything whatsoever as being real, your devotion, pure perception, and compassion may decrease. Not falling prey to the obstacle of emptiness rising as an enemy is thus vitally important.

At this point, seeing the essence of Simplicity depends on whether or not the defilement or conviction of experiences that fixate on emptiness have been purified. The perfection of the training depends upon whether or not you are free from hope and fear or have cut through your misconceptions concerning what is perceived and what is empty. Whether or not thoughts have arisen as meditation depends upon whether or not the realization of the meditation state of recognizing the natural face of all thought occurrences as being nothing but emptiness occurs during the ensuing experience and sleep. The arising of virtuous qualities depends upon whether or not you are connected with the manifest aspect of signs of accomplishment such as the twelve times one hundred qualities of perceiving the truth, that which is to be realized. Mastery over the relative and the sowing of the seed of the rupakaya depend upon whether or not you can arrange the coincidence of bodhichitta and aspiration after having attained certainty in how the manifestation of emptiness arises as cause and effect. It is taught that you should know these dividing points.

One Taste

After having perfected the realization of Simplicity, you understand that designations and distinctions of dualistic attributes such as samsara and nirvana, appearance and emptiness, development and completion, relative and absolute, and so forth all are of One Taste in Mahamudra. Although you are able to condense all the possible attributes of the path into self-knowing, as long as you retain a slight fixation on this experience or some attachment to a conviction about self-knowing, it is called the lesser One Taste.

Having purified the fixation on this experience, you attain the realization of appearance and mind as being inseparable, not even fixating on a separate existence of an actual object to be realized and of the awareness that realizes it. Thus, the medium One Taste is liberation from the duality of perceiver and perceived.

By the power of the multiplicity of all phenomena appearing as One Taste, the expansion of the great expression of wakefulness, the realization of One Taste itself manifesting as multiplicity, is the greater One Taste.

All the forefathers of the Practice Lineage have taught that the genuine mingling of meditation and postmeditation occurs at this point. In other words, any appearance or thought arising is, from the aspect of its essence, primordially dharmakaya or Mahamudra. But in the aspect of its manifestation or as it appears to a deluded person it still retains such characteristics as solid existence and subject-object fixation. It is in fact self-liberated the moment it is embraced by self-knowing mindfulness, a quality not present in the lower yogas.

The moment of embracing a thought with mindfulness in this context means simply allowing whatever manifests or occurs to arise without having to be mindful of or to recognize some essence separate from that. This happening depends on whether or not the essence of One Taste has been seen. Whether or not the training is perfected lies in whether a subtle clinging to an antidote remains or whether One Taste has arisen as multiplicity. "Thought arising as meditation" depends upon whether or not the perceptions of the six senses occurring unimpededly have transcended bondage and liberation. The arising of qualities depends upon whether or not wisdom knowledge has attained mastery over all outer and inner phenomena and has acquired the power to make apparitions, transformations and miracles. Mastery over the relative depends upon whether or not the coincidence of realizing One Taste arising as multiplicity through the mingling of appearance and mind, the cause and effect of mastering appearance and existence has been brought onto the path. The sowing of the seed of the rupakaya depends upon whether or not the treasury of benefit for others has been opened through the power of all-embracing and effortless compassion. Many such statements have been made.

Nonmeditation

When after this you have perfected One Taste, dualistic experiences, such as deliberately meditating or not meditating, being distracted or undistracted, are purified, and you are liberated into the great primordial state in which all experiences are meditation. Lesser Nonmeditation, however, is the arising of merely subtle illusory fixation and tendencies during the night as well as during the ensuing experience.

Medium Nonmeditation is when this illusory fixation is utterly purified, after which the continuity of day and night becomes a single great meditation state and thus the innate nature is realized. But, the presence of a subtle aspect of consciousness as self-knowing, the inherent cover of wakefulness, is itself the defilement of dualistic knowledge. So, not being free from that is the medium Nonmeditation.

When this lack of recognition of nonthought, this subtle obscuration of dualistic knowledge that is like a remnant of the all-ground consciousness, has been completely purified, the luminosity of mother and child mingle together and everything ripens into an all-encompassing expanse of wakefulness, the single circle of dharmakaya. This, the greater Nonmeditation, also called perfect and complete buddhahood, is the arrival at the ultimate fruition.

Seeing the essence of Nonmeditation is nothing but the simple realization of what has become evident at the stage of One Taste, and therefore depends upon whether or not the mind experiencing an object of meditation or familiarization has been purified. Perfecting the training of Nonmeditation depends upon whether or not all defilements of ignorance, the most subtle tendencies of dualistic knowledge, have been exhausted in the wakefulness of realization. Thought arising as meditation depends on whether or not the tendencies of the all-ground have dissolved into the state of dharmadhatu wisdom. The arising of qualities depends on whether or not materiality is manifest as or liberated into the rainbow body, mind into dharmakaya, and the realms into all-encompassing purity. Actualization of the seed of rupakaya depends on whether or not the inexhaustible adornment wheel of Body, Speech and Mind effortlessly accomplishes the welfare of beings throughout space. The purification of all aspects of relative phenomena into dharmadhatu depends upon whether the supreme qualities of buddhahood have been perfected. The Kagyu forefathers have indeed elucidated these and other distinctions.

Summary

As for the meaning of the above condensed into its essence, One-pointedness means being able to remain in meditation for as long as you desire. Simplicity means recognizing your natural face as ordinary mind and realizing it to be devoid of ground and root. One taste means that the dualistic fixation of samsara and nirvana is liberated within awareness. Nonmeditation means that all defilements of conviction and habitual tendencies are purified. The essence of the four yogas is included within this.

In particular, the distinction between the meditation and post-meditation of One-pointedness lies in abiding and not abiding. The distinction between the meditation and post-meditation of Simplicity lies in being or not being mindful. Beyond One Taste, meditation and post-meditation are intermingled; so there is no distinction.

Moreover, the nature of thought arising as nonthought is One-pointedness, arising as emptiness is Simplicity, arising as equality is One Taste, and arising as transcendence of conceptual mind is Nonmeditation.

Furthermore, at the time of One-pointedness, confusion arises uncontrolled; at Simplicity it is realized as devoid of ground and root. At the time of One Taste confusion dawns as wisdom; and the stage of Nonmeditation is beyond the words confusion and non-confusion.

It is further taught that the highest achievement at the time of One-pointedness is realizing the inseparability of stillness and thought occurrence. For Simplicity perfection or the highest achievement is realizing the inseparability of confusion and liberation. For One Taste, it is realizing the inseparability of appearance and mind. And for Nonmeditation, it is realizing the inseparability of meditation and post-meditation.

Moreover, it is taught that One-pointedness is when your mind is grasping at solidity; the state of mind of Simplicity is meditation and post-meditation; the state of mind of One Taste is unity; and Nonmeditation is when your mind is realized.

Lastly, at the time of One-pointedness thoughts are subdued; at the time of Simplicity the root of thoughts is cut; at the time of One Taste self-existing wakefulness dawns from within; and Nonmeditation is the attainment of stability.

Briefly, the different types of distinctions and classifications are certainly of an inexpressible and inexhaustible number, but the definite key point of utmost importance is as follows. Having recognized the innate mode of mind, the natural state exactly as it is, the fact of knowing how to sustain the spontaneous way of ordinary mind, naturalness unspoiled by mental fabrication, is alone important. The wisdom dakini Niguma said:

> If you don't understand that whatever appears is
> meditation,
> What can you achieve by applying an antidote?
> Perceptions are not abandoned by discarding
> them,
> But are spontaneously freed when recognized as
> illusory.

THE FIVE PATHS AND
TEN BHUMIS

Most people nowadays pretending to be Dharma practitioners are chained tightly by the bonds of the eight worldly concerns and, merely pursuing material things and the gain of further possessions, have no thought other than for the food, clothing and pleasures of this life. Some intoxicate themselves with the poison of pride, boasting of a vast learning and knowledge of words but fail to gain mastery over their own minds. Some do aspire toward practicing the definitive meaning but lack an authentic master and the genuine oral instructions. Hence, they imprison themselves within a rigid meditative asceticism—not knowing the practice of all-pervasive openness. Many ignorant meditators earn themselves the prize of *soglung*.

In these times, when mountains and valleys are filled with so-called meditators who perpetuate misdeeds and lack substance—like a stew made of lungs or are hollow like a blacksmith's fan—one may expound upon the qualities of the four yogas, but it will amount to nothing more than telling about the qualities of water in the desert. There is not much point in that.

The fortunate men and women who have definitely given rise to flawless experience and realization do not depend on external words and letters when the knowledge resulting from meditation has arisen from within. Therefore, they surely have no need for lengthy explanations from someone like myself, which are like narrations of a place far away by a person who has not been there himself.

A well-gifted and qualified person who is endowed with perseverance, who follows a perfect master and, having received the blessings, can practice steadfastly, will, with regard to the manifestation of the experiences and realizations of the respective four yogas described above, automatically journey through the progressive stages of the five paths and ten bhumis of the general vehicles in their entirety. The *King of Samadhi Sutra* says:

> The person who adheres to this supreme
> samadhi
> And who upholds its teaching will, wherever he
> goes
> Have gentle behavior and be utterly at peace.
> The Joyous, the Stainless, and the Radiant,
> The Brilliant, the Hard to Conquer, and the
> Realized bhumi,
> The Reaching Far, the Unshakable, and the
> Good Intelligence,
> The Cloud of Dharma—thus he will attain the
> ten bhumis.

The Five Paths

In other words, on the lesser, medium, and higher stages of the path of accumulation you achieve the four applications of mindfulness, the four right exertions, and the four legs of miraculous action. They all are complete within this swift oral instruction path of Mahamudra in the following way:

First of all, the general preliminaries are the reflection on the sufferings of samsara, the difficult to find freedoms and riches, the impermanence of life, and so forth. These aspects completely contain the four applications of mindfulness: mindfulness of the body as impure, mindfulness of sensations as painful, mindfulness of mind as impermanent, and mindfulness of phenomena as devoid of self-entity. Concentrating on the key points of these preliminaries, and gaining some experience or certainty in them, is therefore called traversing the lesser path of accumulation.

Similarly, the four right exertions of not producing unvirtuous qualities, abandoning those that have arisen, developing virtuous qualities, and increasing the ones that have arisen, are in this context all included within taking refuge, arousing bodhichitta, the Hundred Syllables, and the mandala offerings, which therefore are called traversing the medium path of accumulation.

Following that, guru yoga includes the four legs of miraculous action: engendering one-pointed devotion to the guru is the miraculous leg of determination.

Receiving the four empowerments is the leg of discernment. Supplicating is the leg of diligence. And finally mingling the guru and one's own mind together is the miraculous leg of concentration. Through them you traverse the greater path of accumulation.

The paramita vehicle teaches that the qualities of having perfected the path of accumulation are that you can journey to pure realms and meet the nirmanakaya buddhas in person and so forth. In this context, the eminent master is the essence of all the three kayas of buddhahood and his field of conversion is no other than a nirmanakaya realm; this, therefore, is in harmony with the above meaning.

The lesser, medium and higher stages at the time of One-pointedness are the path of joining, which includes the four aspects of ascertainment*: Seeing the essence of mind is called heat; gaining certainty therein is called summit; being unharmed by circumstances is acceptance; and being uninterrupted in one-pointed practice is called the supreme mundane quality of the path of joining.

At this time you also gain the specific qualities of the five faculties: Gaining boundless certainty is the faculty of faith. Looking into the nature undistractedly is the faculty of mindfulness. Not being interrupted by laziness is the faculty of diligence. Being uninterrupted in meditation is the faculty of concentration. Realizing

---

* The four aspects of ascertainment (nges 'byed bzhi): heat (drod), summit (rtse mo), acceptance (bzod pa), and supreme mundane quality ('jig rten chos mchog).

the definitive meaning is the faculty of discriminating knowledge.

These five faculties having become individually perfected or turned into a strength are also called the five strengths.

Having in this way realized the three stages of One-pointedness, you have perfected the path of joining and arrived at Simplicity. Because of seeing the truth of a realization which was not seen earlier, you have attained the path of seeing.

The paramita vehicle teaches that at this point one cultivates the seven bodhi-factors; in this context they are automatically present. In other words, abiding in the state of dharmata, the natural state as it is, is the bodhi-factor of samadhi. Not to be mixed with disturbing emotions is the bodhi-factor of fully discerning phenomena. Since the defilements to be relinquished through the path of seeing are naturally purified simply by remembering this samadhi, this is the bodhi-factor of mindfulness. Being freed from laziness and distraction, this is the bodhi-factor of diligence. Since you enjoy unconditioned bliss, this is the bodhi-factor of joy. Since all objects to be relinquished are purified, this is the bodhi-factor of pliancy. Because of realizing samsara and nirvana to be equality, this is the bodhi-factor of impartiality. Thus are the seven bodhi-factors perfected.

It is further taught that you attain the numerous qualities of the path of seeing as well as infinite samadhi doors.

Some masters hold that the path of cultivation and the first bhumi have been attained at the moment of perfecting the three stages of Simplicity and arriving at One Taste. Most other masters accept that the attainment of the first bhumi is exactly the post-meditation after having seen the essence of Simplicity and given rise to the path of seeing. The different levels of individual capacity obviously make fixed generalizations impossible. It is thus unquestionable that there are various types of scope and speed in traversing the paths.

The genuine realization of the path of seeing arising in this way is called *bhumi* since it is the source of or forms the basis for all good qualities. The *Avatamsaka Sutra* teaches:

> As soon as the bhumi is attained you are free
>   from five fears:
> Free from fear of harm, of death, or of falling
>   into the lower realms,
> Free from fear of being in samsara, and free
>   from anxiety.

In this way, the qualities of the ten bhumis increase further and further.

The period following the attainment of the bhumi is called the path of cultivation. Why is that? The path of cultivation is so called because you accustom yourself to the nature of the path of seeing.

At this point, you engage in the eightfold noble path. On this path of cultivation, in the meditation state you cultivate exclusively an unconditioned samadhi and in the ensuing experience the eight aspects of the noble path which are regarded as conditioned. What are these eight? They are right view, thought, speech, conduct, livelihood, effort, mindfulness, and right concentration. In short, being nothing but accomplishments of a perfect nature, they are fully endowed with numerous qualities which are especially exalted above the steps of the path below.

The Ten Bhumis

The first of the ten bhumis is called the Joyous because of taking great delight in the special qualities. By means of the meditation state, which is nonconceptual nonarising and the post-meditation state, which is illusory, you traverse the path chiefly through practicing the paramita of generosity with a frame of mind free from dread or faint-heartedness even when sacrificing your head or limbs and so forth for the sake of sentient beings. In this way the general vehicle indeed has extensive details teaching the ten paramitas combined with the ten bhumis in progressive order. In this context they are as follows.

Since at the first stage of Simplicity the joy of samadhi is greatly increased, you reach the first bhumi of the Joyful. Being free from the defilements of what is to be relinquished through the path of cultivation, you reach the second bhumi of the Stainless. Accomplishing the welfare of beings through the power of realization, you reach the third bhumi of the Radiant.

At the medium stage of Simplicity, the supreme buddha qualities being further increased, you reach the fourth bhumi of the Brilliant. Because of purifying all the defilements of the tendencies that are difficult to purify through having realized emptiness and compassion as a unity, you reach the fifth bhumi of the Hard to Conquer.

At the time of realizing the Greater Simplicity, due to realizing samsara and nirvana to be nonarising, you reach the sixth bhumi of the Realized. The bhumis up to this point are taught as being common to those of the shravakas and pratyekabuddhas.

Following this, dualistic experiences such as meditation and post-meditation, samsara and nirvana, are for the most part liberated as a unity and thus the beginning of this realization of One Taste is the seventh bhumi of Reaching Far.

Unmoved from the correct mindfulness of what is to be realized, you are at the medium One Taste, the eighth bhumi of the Unshakable. When the remaining defilements except for the very subtle, such as the illusory dualistic experience, are purified, you are at the higher stage of One Taste, the ninth bhumi of Good Intelligence.

When this subtle dualistic experience is also naturally purified, all the qualities of the paths and bhumis have been perfected. There still remains, however, the obscuration of dualistic knowledge which is the habitual tendency for fixation, an extremely subtle defilement of the remainder of the all-ground consciousness. It is, in this context, the time of the lesser and medium stages of Nonmeditation, which according to the general system is called the tenth bhumi of the Cloud of Dharma. Up to this point, you possess qualities equal in status to the bodhisattva lords of the ten bhumis.

Buddhahood

The defilement of not knowing the nonconceptual nature, the subtle tendency for dualistic knowledge, then also dissolves into great self-existing self-knowing, the essence of vajralike wakefulness, and you are permanently free from all obscurations. The power of the wakefulness of the nature as it is and of all that exists, as well as the strength of knowledge, compassion, and capacity are fully perfected. The outer and general vehicles describe this point as the supreme path of completion, the actual state of perfect buddhahood which here, in the context of Mahamudra, is called the greater Nonmeditation.

According to the general Secret Mantra, you are now free from the obscurations of karma, disturbing emotions, and habitual tendencies and have therefore no more path to train in, traverse or realize. But in terms of the particular degree of increase in qualities, there is the eleventh bhumi of the Universal Light and the twelfth bhumi of the Lotus of Nonattachment. Having from one moment to the next realized these two extraordinary inner bhumis, the rupakayas for the benefit of others as the expression of having perfected dharmakaya for the benefit of yourself, you then continuously accomplish the great welfare of beings throughout space for as long as samsara has not been emptied. That is called the thirteenth bhumi of the Vajra Holder, buddhahood itself.

As long as these paths and bhumis have something higher to journey towards, they are called the path of learning. Reaching the ultimate where there is no higher place to travel to, is called the path of non-learning. Thus the thirteenth bhumi of the Vajra Holder is the final fruition of the inner Secret Mantra.

The Qualities

What special qualities accompany the attainment of these bhumis? Attaining the first bhumi you can journey simultaneously to one hundred nirmanakaya realms in the ten directions, see one hundred buddhas in person, and hear the Dharma. You can simultaneously perform one hundred different acts of generosity, such as sacrificing even life and limb, kingdom, children and wife without second thoughts. You can simultaneously emanate one hundred different rays of light, radiating red light while absorbing white light, sending forth yellow light while being encircled in blue light, emanating many while re-absorbing a few and so forth. You can simultaneously teach one-hundred Dharma-doors, each in conformity with the individual dispositions, capacities, and inclinations of one hundred different disciples. You can simultaneously enter one hundred different samadhis such as the Courageous Movement, the Subjugating, and the Majestic Lion, which have been taught in the Prajnaparamita by the Victorious One. You can simultaneously show one hundred different kinds of miraculous displays such as flying through the sky or moving through the earth, going unimpededly through mountains or rocks and not sinking down into water. You can also send forth flames from the upper part of the body and water from the lower or vice versa, as well as creating apparitions and transformations of letting one appear as many forms or absorbing many into one. These are the seven times one hundred qualities over which you gain mastery.

Likewise, in progression, you will, on the second bhumi have seven times one thousand of these qualities, on the third seven times ten thousand, on the fourth seven times one hundred thousand, on the fifth seven times one million, on the sixth seven times ten million, on the seventh seven times one hundred millions, on the eighth seven times one billion, on the ninth seven times ten billion, on the tenth seven times one hundred billion, on the eleventh seven times one trillion, and on the twelfth seven times ten trillion. On realizing the thirteenth bhumi of the Vajra Holder, the nature of the three kayas of buddhahood, the number of supreme qualities is infinite. This nature transcends the limits of conceptual thinking and can be measured by no one.

How the Qualities Manifest

This path of Mahamudra, the pinnacle of the vehicles, contains the ten bhumis and five paths taught in the general vehicles in their entirety and without being mixed together. The nature of things therefore is that a person who correctly realizes the four yogas will gradually or instantaneously perfect all the qualities of these paths and bhumis. For some people these qualities are, however, not superficially present to be perceived as something concretely visible. That is the nature of the hidden short path of the Secret Mantra. Most birds and wild animals after being born from their mother's womb must yet develop their bodily strength to gradually become equal to their mother. The garuda bird, ruler of the feathered race, or on the other hand the lion, king of the wild animals, perfects its strength within the egg or the womb where it is indeed not perceived by others. Once born, by the power of having fully perfected its strength, it is immediately able to act on its own, such as flying together with its mother through the skies.

Similarly, the signs of realization do not visibly manifest as long as the practitioner remains encased within his material body; later however, with the disintegration of the bodily encasement and the ripening of fruition, perfection of the qualities, will occur simultaneously.

Nonetheless, many people, concentrating on the key points of the path of united means and knowledge, visibly manifest within their very bodies the signs of the path such as the miracles and superknowledges. But in actuality, without having attained mastery over the sameness of space and wakefulness, the mind beyond conceptual thinking, the natural state of the essence of things and the true innate wakefulness, some so-called siddhas are possessed by the demon of arrogance and become overjoyed by, cling to as excellent, and regard as supreme the mere fragments of signs of attainment in the practices of development and completion, of the channels, winds and essences, and so forth. They only herd themselves and others into the lower realms. They are abundant nowadays; so beware, all intelligent people!

ENHANCEMENT

Having in this way briefly described the view and meditation, the paths and the bhumis, I shall also explain in short how to practice the conduct, the application of enhancement.

According to most paths of Secret Mantra, the different types of conduct mentioned are the three of elaborate, unelaborate, and very unelaborate conduct. There are also secret conduct, group conduct, awareness discipline, the completely victorious conduct and so forth. Many such categories exist, but they are for the most part general enhancements for the stages of development and completion. In this context, the ever-excellent conduct, sustaining the natural mode of the innate, free from conceptual mind, is alone important.

First of all, even during the preliminary stages of gathering the accumulations, purifying the obscurations, and the means for receiving the blessings, you should exert yourself in practicing the ever-excellent conduct of being untainted by the defilement of any of the eight worldly concerns and of not feeling ashamed of yourself.

Next, when gaining certainty about the view and meditation of the main part of practice and becoming clear about self-knowing, you should exert yourself in the ever-excellent conduct of being skilled in all by knowing one and knowing all that liberates one. That is the means of "hammering down the nails" of many plans from within yourself and cutting through the arrogance of doubt in your own mind.

Finally, although various authoritative scriptures and oral instructions have taught different types of conduct as means to enhance one's practice, the essential key points are as follows: Cut your worldly attachments completely and live companionless in secluded mountain retreats; that is the conduct of a wounded deer. Be free from fear or anxiety in the face of difficulties; that is the conduct of a lion sporting in the mountains. Be free from attachment or clinging to sense pleasures; that is the conduct of the wind in the sky. Do not become involved in the fetters of accepting or rejecting the eight worldly concerns; that is the conduct of a madman. Sustain simply and unrestrictedly the natural flow of your mind while unbound by the ties of dualistic fixation; that is the conduct of a spear stabbing in space.

While engaging in these types of conduct, cut the fetters of deluded wandering, distraction, hope and fear. Becoming involved in even as much as a hair tip of the inner fault of desiring to have signs and indications, experience and realization, or siddhis and so forth, will gain you nothing but obscuring your real condition, your innate state, the natural face of dharmakaya. Focus exclusively on sustaining the unconstructed innate nature; that is the most eminent Ever-Excellent conduct of bringing things into the path.

Regardless of what various difficulties such as conceptual thinking, disturbing emotions, suffering, fear, sickness or death temporarily occur, be able to bring these into the path as the main part of the natural Mahamudra practice, neither hoping for nor relying on some other means of benefit through an antidote. That is the king of all types of enhancement.

The person able to practice like this will gain mastery over all of samsara and nirvana, appearance and existence. So, the nature of things is that you will be free from any basis of obstacles, the great ocean of siddhis will overflow, the darkness of the two obscurations will be cleared, the sun of signs of accomplishment will shines forth, the buddha will be discovered within your own mind, and the treasury of benefiting others will be opened wide.

It is, on the contrary, indeed cause for despair to see the meditators who seem to be exclusively throwing away the single sufficient jewel that has been placed in their hands, and like a child picking flowers they spend a lifetime wishing for one better thing to do after another.

Section Three

FRUITION MAHAMUDRA

THE THREE KAYAS OF
BUDDHAHOOD

Having briefly described the nature of the ground and the path, the view, meditation, and conduct, I shall now conclude with the third major point: explaining the meaning of fruition Mahamudra, the inseparability of the three kayas or the unity of the two kayas.

Dharmakaya

When a gifted practitioner has seen the natural face of ground Mahamudra, the innate state and, focusing on the key points of practicing path Mahamudra, the view and meditation, has reached perfection in the training, he has at this point realized the final fruition Mahamudra, the ultimate dharmakaya.

The essence of dharmakaya is self-knowing and unfabricated original wakefulness, unchanging and free from increase or decrease, primordially present in the mind-stream of all sentient beings of the three realms. This is exactly what is to be realized through the means of practice, the profound key points of the path. Besides this wakefulness there is nothing other, no new or unprec-

edented buddha or dharmakaya that is to appear. The
characteristics of dharmakaya are as follows.

Being endowed with the wakefulness of knowing the
nature as it is and with the wakefulness of all existent
objects of knowledge, it is called endowed with the twofold
knowledge. Since the essence is primordially and utterly
pure and since the passing, coemergent defilements are
purified, dharmakaya is also said to be endowed with the
twofold purity. Actually, it is free from the defilement of
not knowing or not perceiving all knowable phenomena
and has fully perfected all aspects of good qualities.

This dharmakaya's unobstructed expression of manifestation, the display of this wakefulness, gives rise to the
two kayas of sambhogakaya and nirmanakaya.

Seven Aspects of Unity

These three kayas possess the qualities of being endowed
with the seven aspects of unity. What are these seven?

(1) The aspect of enjoyment is due to perpetually and
continually utilizing the Dharma-wheels of the profound,
the extensive, and the Secret Mantra for all the great
bodhisattvas in the abode of Akanishtha. (2) The aspect
of union is due to the wisdom body of perfect marks and
signs being united with the consort of its natural radiance.
(3) The aspect of great bliss is due to unconditioned great
bliss being unceasing. These three are the special attributes of sambhogakaya. (4) The aspect of being totally

filled with compassion is nonconceptual compassion, all-encompassing like space. (5) The aspect of continuity is the occurrence, spontaneously and without concepts, of vast activity equal to the limits of samsara. (6) The aspect of uninterruptedness is the nondwelling on the peaceful extreme of nirvana. These three are the special attributes of nirmanakaya. (7) The aspect of absence of self-nature, since the unity of emptiness and compassion is totally free from mental constructs and thus devoid of a self-nature, is regarded as the special attribute of dharmakaya. In this way the three kayas are endowed with seven aspects.

Eight Masteries of Sambhogakaya

It is also taught that they possess the eight qualities of mastery:

(1) Being endowed with all the aspects of taming whoever needs in whichever way is necessary is the mastery of body. (2) The unceasing wheel of Dharma to tame whomever is in need is the mastery of speech. (3) Possessing nonconceptual compassion is the mastery of mind. (4) Unimpeded miraculous powers are the mastery of miracles. (5) The true enlightenment of samsara and nirvana and the three times as being equal and of one taste is the mastery of all-pervasiveness. (6) Being untainted by desire even when presented with sense pleasures by offering goddesses equal in number to the dust motes of thirty-two Sumerus is the mastery of desire. (7) Fulfilling

the desires and hopes of beings in accordance with their wishes as does a wishfulfilling gem is the mastery of granting whatever is desired. (8) Abiding continually as the Dharma King over the three realms in the dharmadhatu palace of Akanishtha is the mastery of abode. Possessing the eight masteries is one description of the qualities of sambhogakaya.

Nirmanakaya

The nirmanakayas are emanated as the inconceivable manifestation of dharmakaya and sambhogakaya. Thus emanated to tame beings, these reflections of the moon correspond to the number of vessels of water where they appear. The appearance of infinite and numberless emanations to tame whoever is in need in whichever way is necessary, be it through the nirmanakayas of creation, of incarnation, or of great enlightenment and so forth, is known as the inexhaustible adornment wheel of the secrets of the Body, Speech, and Mind of all the buddhas.

The Causes for Accomplishing the Kayas

The actual fruition of focusing on the key point of the ultimate emptiness of Mahamudra right now at the time of the path is the accomplishment of dharmakaya. As the subsidiary part of that, the aspect of means, you will accomplish nirmanakaya purely through the power of developing bodhichitta, making aspirations and so forth. You attain the sambhogakaya through the causation of having practiced the profound development stage. Thus through the power of endeavoring in these practices, not in a differentiated or sporadic way but as the unity of means and knowledge, the great and complete threefold purity, you will attain stability in the essence within which the three kayas are inseparable.

The three kayas explained here as well as the numerous classifications of four or five kayas are one identity with different names given to the various qualities or functions. They are in short nothing other than the present essence, nature, and expression of your mind which, at the time of fruition, are called the three kayas.

Summary

In this context, the causal vehicles and the lower tantras of Mantra contain numberless commentaries and systems which adhere to particular points of view as well as quotations intended for another purpose or with a concealed intent: whether or not dharmakaya has a face and arms; whether its realm is demonstrable or not demonstrable; whether or not a buddha has wisdom comprised of his own stream-of-being; and whether or not the two rupakayas have sensation as personal experience, and so forth.

These many subjects of debate along with their proofs and refutations indeed seem complicated. But while these topics are all surely valid each in its own context, here, in the quintessence of vehicles, one need not depend upon establishing the views of the lower vehicles.

The meaning here is known as "in harmony with all yet exalted above them." What does this meaning intend? Do not apprehend, do not cling to, do not refute, and do not establish any of all the phenomena comprising samsara and nirvana, appearance and existence, as being either real or unreal, existent or nonexistent, true or untrue, arising or ceasing, coming or going, permanent or annihilated. One who holds them to be nonexistent falls into the extreme of nihilism, and one who holds them to be existent falls into the extreme of eternalism. Thinking, "They are neither existent nor nonexistent!" also does not transcend mental fabrication. So if something exists in the experience of others, then let it exist because unobstructed perception is inexhaustible, and the coincidence of causation is unfailing. If something is nonexistent in the perception of others, then let it be nonexistent since in essence it has never moved away from emptiness, the nature of possessing no existence whatsoever. If something is held to be neither existent nor nonexistent, then let that also be true as it falls into neither extreme and is also not confined to any category of classification.

All things appearing as the external world and beings are perceived by impure sentient beings' deluded habitual tendencies and karmic experiences as the material and solid five elements. Practitioners on the path perceive all things as the unceasing display of their own minds. The buddhas and bodhisattvas perceive things as the realms of self-manifest wakefulness. Ultimately, everything is no more than the magical display of the mind-essence.

Similarly, all the inner cognitive acts and thoughts of the mental states are, for impure deluded beings, of the nature of karma, disturbing emotions, and habitual tendencies. For practitioners on the path, cognitive acts are the different aspects of the view and meditation, experience and realization. Finally, for the sugata buddhas of the three kayas, cognitive acts are the wisdom display of knowledge and loving kindness.

Although not even an atom of difference exists in the natural state of the ground, the difference lies in whether it is totally enveloped in the passing conceptual obscurations (as in the case of all sentient beings), whether it is slightly covered (as in the case of practitioners on the path), or whether it is free from obscurations (as in the case of the buddhas).

The key point of sole importance is therefore to relax into the state of Mahamudra, your own unfabricated mind, the essential nature that has never been transcended (since the primordial beginning), is not transcending (in the present), and will never transcend (in the future) the essence of ground, path and fruition, the union of the two kayas, or the indivisibility of the three kayas.

Those who form exaggerations and denigrations about the unconditioned nature with their conditioned intellects, who cling to the limitations of words and argue while adhering to partisan philosophical schools are childish trying to grasp the extent of the sky. Rest therefore in great all-pervasive equality in the expanse of unconstructed naturalness. There is then no doubt that, beyond the concepts of journey and traveler, you will be liberated into the nature endowed with the spontaneously present fruition of the four yogas, the ten bhumis, the five paths and the three kayas.

Epilogue

Kyeho!
The nature of sugata-essence, originally free
    since the beginning,
The buddhahood of the spontaneously present
    three kayas,
Is in all beings down to the tiniest insect,
Always present without separation though
    obscured by ignorance.

Though Dharma-doors equal in number to those
    to be tamed are taught to tame beings,
They remain deluded by their impure personal
    perceptions,
On mistaken paths, wrong paths, errant paths,
    and fettered by their paths;
To journey the excellent and perfect path is as
    rare as the udumbara flower.

Chained in fixation on extremes while
    transcending extremes (the view)
Not recognized, like the treasure of a destitute,
    while present in oneself, (the meditation)
Spoiled by fabrication while self-manifesting and
    unfabricated, (the action)

What a great blunder not recognizing the nature
of things as they are!

The powerful and wealthy become obsessed with
their merit.
People bloated with learning become hardened
like butter-skin.
Ignorant meditators persevere in rigidity, as if
trying to press oil from sand,
Who then is endowed with Mahamudra of the
natural state?

Alas!
The supreme teaching of Sutra and Tantra, like
the pair of the sun and the moon,
Is now only partly present,
As the vermilion glow on clouds after the sunset
in the west;
What is the point in casting freedoms and riches
in the gutter for this life's sake?

Living in unpeopled mountain hermitages,
Relying merely on simple food to support one's
life
While looking into the innate natural face, the
eminent permanent goal;
Is this not the tradition of the Practice Lineage?

Nowadays deeds claimed to benefit the teachings
cause its degeneration,

And endeavor is not for attaining the genuine
 truth;
Who will need and who will appreciate
These sporadic writings by someone like me?

I may fill my room with pages of scribbles
Not needed by myself and not appreciated by
 others.
Incapable of taming the mind of even one
 person,
They are naught but paper, ink and tiring labor
 for my fingers.

Unable to refuse the request
Of someone who for a long time has insistently
 pleaded,
I have uttered this simply from
 presumptuousness,
While it lacks any power of a flawless
 composition of words with consistent
 meaning.

Lacking discernment that masters the expressing
 word
As well as experience of having realized the great
 expressed meaning,
How can this composition
Possibly become anything more than a laughing
 stock for learned and accomplished beings?

Nevertheless, this beautiful garland of
  blossoming white lotuses,
Illuminated by a noble motivation and
  unobscured by evil intent,
May just possibly become an ornament for the
  ears
Of some simple aspirant meditators like myself.

By the merit of having written this
Combined with all conditioned and
  unconditioned virtue of samsara, nirvana,
  and the path,
May the Practice Lineage teachings flourish
  throughout all directions,
And may all beings realize the fruition of
  Mahamudra.

For a long time I was repeatedly requested by Tsültrim Zangpo, the vidyadhara of Mengom, in these words: "Please write a detailed and extensive textbook of necessary instructions on enhancement and the signs of the stages of the path for practitioners of the Mahamudra of definitive meaning." But as an endless number of these types of books, both profound and extensive, exist in the collected works of the forefathers of the Practice Lineage, there was no need to compose another.

However, I have indeed been considered with affection by many kind refuge masters and have received the following works on the profound path of Mahamudra:

Uniting with the Coemergent, The Four Words, Gangama, The Letterless, the teachings on the *Root of Symbols* and the *Essence of Accomplishment*, the *Inconceivable Secret, The Illuminating Wisdom, The Fivefold*, the *Wishfulfilling Jewel*, the *Six Nails of Key Points*, as well as numerous other teachings of direct instructions famed among the New Schools. From the Old School teaching, I have kindly been given the *Mahamudra of Unconfined Vastness*, the *Circle of the Sun*, the *Single Arisen Awareness, Dispelling the Darkness of Ignorance, Directly Seeing the Innate*, as well as numerous other works of revealed termas.

Despite receiving all these teachings, I possess no ability or courage to compose such a work. Having been tossed about on the waves of karma, disturbing emotions, and distraction, consequently not even the tiniest fraction of experience or realization of their meaning has arisen within my mind.

However, I beg wholeheartedly that all intelligent people will not despise these writings made by a blind man in a dense darkness simply in order not to turn down the word of the one who asked me.

By the virtue of this may all beings throughout space, my past mothers, attain within this very lifetime the sublime state of unexcelled enlightenment.

May it be virtuous!

May it be virtuous!

May it be virtuous!

The Heart of
the Matter

INTRODUCTION

The perfect Buddha Shakyamuni gave us, his disciples, boundless Dharma Wheels each in accordance with our various capacities and inclinations. The quintessence of all these teachings is the third turning of the Dharma Wheel, called the "final set of teachings on the complete and total uncovering." This is the Vajrayana approach to the definitive meaning that takes the fruition as the path, wherein the crucial points of how to apply its view and meditation training are shown. The know-how for bringing this definitive meaning into our experience is found in a text entitled *The Unchanging Convergence*, which here, in English, is called *The Heart of the Matter*.

The author, Tsele Natsok Rangdröl, was born in the snowy land of Tibet. It was through study and reflection that he first unraveled the key points of everything that there is to know. Having brought forth realization through meditation training, he became known as a great pandita and siddha, a learned and accomplished master.

Among his various instructions, *The Heart of the Matter* is both concise and comprehensible. Not only does it contain all the vital points of the Buddha's words but, in particular, it lucidly and precisely covers the definitive meaning of the view, meditation, conduct and fruition, in their entirety, so that their practice can take effect and mature in our minds.

I feel that *The Heart of the Matter* contains extremely precious and crucial advice. Since it is now available in English, I pray that everyone who wishes to sincerely practice the flawless teachings of the Buddha may take its meaning to heart and apply it correctly. This will not only eliminate all shortcomings within you but will also allow you to accurately realize your intrinsic wakefulness, the true natural state present within all of us. This is no other than the view of Mahamudra, Dzogchen and the Middle Way. May you quickly attain the unified state of Vajradhara!

Please appreciate that this book is a pith instruction, a direct path which is complete and unmistaken. Try to assimilate its meaning in your hearts to the best of your ability. Sarva mangalam—may it be auspicious!

Chökyi Nyima Rinpoche

Svasti Prajnabhya

To the awakened mind, utterly pure since the
    beginning,
The uncontrived innate, the coemergent
    dharmakaya,
Which is the nature of all things, inconceivable
    in number,
I bow down by realizing the spontaneously
    present guru of natural awareness.

Sugata-essence is present as the nature of all
    beings,
But due to coemergent ignorance,
They constantly obscure themselves and sink
    into the ocean of samsara.
So to quickly liberate them, I shall now explain
    the innermost, profound path.

With dread for the painful abyss of the lower
    realms,
Without attachment to errant paths, nor to the
    peace of shravakas and pratyekabuddhas,
And with the wish to attain perfect buddhahood
    in a single lifetime,
Wise and most fortunate ones, engage yourselves
    in this practice!

How wonderful is the aspiration of the one with
    that very name,
Who asked me "Please expound upon the key
    points of essential training
In the view and meditation of Mahamudra,
    Dzogchen, and the Middle Way!"
I offer this small token of reply.

The sole purpose of the different turnings of the
    Dharma Wheels
By the victorious ones of the three times
Is to establish sentient beings in the state of
    buddhahood.

But due to the diverse mentalities and fortunes
    of those to be tamed,
The teachings to tame them are also different.
Since all are the activity of the victorious ones,
There are indeed no good or bad teachings.

Nevertheless, by being the support for the path,
    the path itself,
Or connecting you with the fruition in actuality,
The teachings renowned as the lesser, medium
    and greater vehicles
Are all alike in that through them you realize
    enlightenment.

But it is through the special quality of being a
    short path,
That the Greater Vehicle is exceedingly superior.

Yet superior to it, the path of Mantra
Is even higher and amazingly unique.

The ground, path and fruition—
Although these three are taught,
Samsara and nirvana are still indivisible as the
    expanse of the three kayas
And the ground and fruition never depart from
    being one taste.

Even though the ground is free of delusion,
In order to remove the ignorant delusion
Of being momentarily unaware of this fact,
Numerous practices of the path have been
    taught.

Their essence is twofold, comprised of both view
    and meditation;
But first of all, it is of sole importance
To recognize the very meaning of the view.

There are many types of view
Such as the uninformed views of ordinary
    people,
And the misunderstood views of extremist
    philosophies.
As they do not lead to enlightenment
I will not describe them here in detail.
If you desire to know their fine points,
Then look in the many [sutras and] tantras of the
    Old and New Schools

And in all the great treatises.

As for the view of shravakas and
    pratyekabuddhas of Hinayana,
The shravakas understand the absence of
    personal identity
But not of the identity of things,
So they hold on to a solidity of perceived objects.

Through their understanding of emptiness, the
    pratyekabuddhas
Realize that there is no object-identity in the
    perceived,
But fail to realize the absence of object-identity
    in the perceiver,
And therefore are still deluded.

The meditation practice of both shravakas and
    pratyekabuddhas
Is to train in the concentrations and in the
    serenity of cessation.
Though carrying out the five paramitas,
Their conduct is not embraced by vipashyana,
    the paramita of discriminating knowledge,
And therefore it is taught that they are in error.

In the bodhisattva teachings of Mahayana
There are the Mind Only and the Middle Way
    Schools.
The Mind Only has two schools: True Image
    and False Image,

And their view is to claim that samsara and
   nirvana are mind.

The followers of the Svatantrika Middle Way
Accept the unity of the two truths as the view,
While the followers of the Prasangika Middle
   Way
Teach that the view is free from claims.

All of them, however, train after establishing,
By means of discriminating knowledge,
That the meditation is self-aware, natural
   knowing,
The indivisible unity of knowing and emptiness.

Their conduct is to reach accomplishment
   through the ten paramitas
By endeavoring in the twofold welfare of self and
   others.
The fruition, [which only occurs] after three
   incalculable aeons,
Is taught to be the attainment of unexcelled
   enlightenment.

The followers of Outer Mantra such as Kriya
   and Yoga,
Hold the view of purity beyond four limitations.
Their meditation is to train in development
   combined with completion,
And their conduct is to maintain cleanliness and
   honor the deity.

By observing their respective samayas,
It is taught that after seven or sixteen lifetimes,
They attain the five kayas of buddhahood.

The followers of Anuttara, the Inner Secret
    Mantra,
Hold that the view is empty experience, and the
    world and beings are sacred.
Their meditation is passion and deliverance in
    the unity of development and completion,
And is entered through the eminent path of the
    four empowerments.

Through their conduct, such as utterly pure
    activity,
Which is the inconceivable skillful means
Of the general and specific union and liberation,
They attain, in just one lifetime,
The supreme and common fruitions that
    accomplish the benefit of self and others.

These individual stages of view and meditation
On all levels of the vehicles,
Are found in the countless sutras, tantras and
    treatises,
So what is the use of someone like me explaining
    them here?

In general, I am devoid of learning,
And in particular, I have neither studied nor
    reflected on the scriptures,
Including the Middle Way, logic, and
    Prajnaparamita.
So for me to persist, while unacquainted with
    their specific views,
Would only provoke contempt from learned
    people.
Out of sincere interest in the inconceivable
    dharmadhatu,
I will therefore rest my case.

The heart of the matter to be explained here,
Uniformly taught by most learned siddhas of the
    New and Old Schools,
Is that the difference between Mantra and the
    Philosophical Vehicle
Lies not in the view but in practicing
The vital points of skillful means.

There are some who claim a huge difference,
But, this old simpleton has found that
The essential point, the crucial meaning,
Is that—although the nature of the view is the
    same—
Any difference merely lies in forming or not
    forming a conceptual attitude,

Or in having or not having personal opinion and
fixation.

Although no defining characteristics exist in
themselves,
The attempts to establish intellectually,
By scrutiny and conceptualizing,
The various claims that something is empty or
not empty,
And with or without limitations,
Is never taught to be the view of Mahamudra
and Dzogchen,
And to believe "It is free from limits!" or "It is
emptiness!"
Is nothing other than straying from the view.

Rather than holding a view of mind-made
assumptions,
Realize your indescribable and unformed innate
nature,
Through nakedly recognizing self-knowing
wakefulness,
As the basic state of what is.

In the *Noble Eight Thousand Verses* (the Buddha) says:

"Subhuti, that being so, this transcendent knowledge fully remains as inconceivable action and thus

is not the domain of common thought. Why is this? It is because it does not involve the attributes of (dualistic) mind and mental events."

So he taught. Tilopa also mentions:

> Kye ho! This self-knowing wakefulness
> Lies beyond words and the reach of thought.

Maitripa said:

> All phenomena are empty of their own identities.
> The conceptual attitude which holds them to be
>   empty dissolves in itself.
> To be concept-free and hold nothing in mind,
> Is the path of all buddhas.

Shang Rinpoche, the lord of beings, said:

> If you wish to realize the view, the nature of
>   things,
> Do not behold a view, simply cast away the act of
>   viewing.
> When free from the schemes of viewing and not
>   viewing,
> To give up doing is to reach the ultimate view.

Khachö Lutreng said,

> "This is limited! This is free from limitations!"
>   and so forth—
> This view of holding such eminent claims will
>   shroud you in falsehood.
> In the ordinary view of simply what is,
> You see no "thing" and yet it is seen.

He continues:

> The two truths of the learned scholar
> May be full of logic and citations but miss the
>   vital point.
> To split it in two spoils nonduality,
> And forever spins the conceptual machine that
>   accepts and rejects.

There is an untold number of such quotations.

> In the great chariots of the traditions of Maitreya
>   and Manjushri,
> Who unraveled the intents of the middle and
>   final Wheels taught by the Buddha,
> And in the philosophical systems known as the
>   Middle Way and Mind Only,

Of their successors Asanga, Nagarjuna, and so
    forth,
How can there possibly ever be any faults!

Although there is not the slightest disharmony
Between them and the meaning of Mahamudra
    and Dzogchen,
There have been many people in later times
    whose pretense of scholarship
Polluted the Middle Way and Mind Only by
    tainting it with their personal inventions.

Their manifold arguments to prove or disprove
    a maxim,
Regardless of how lofty the understanding of
    such an established view may be,
Will not result in realization of self-existing
    wakefulness, simply as it is,
Let alone enlightenment.
But without reducing disturbing emotions in the
    least,
They swell with intellectual pretension and the
    pride of vast learning,
Heading for disaster by using the Dharma to
    create rebirth in the lower realms.

Saraha, the great brahmin, said:

> Those who don't drink their fill
> From the cool and soothing nectar of their
> master's oral instructions,
> Will only be tortured by thirst
> On the desert plains of countless treatises.

> For this reason, it is essential
> Not to pursue nor cling to views proven only by
> words,
> But to personally begin training in the view and
> meditation
> Of the lineage of profound meaning.

> You may wonder if the prelude to meditation,
> the various ways of seeking the mind,
> Isn't a conceptualized form of analysis.
> Well it isn't, since its source, dwelling and
> disappearance
> Are all realized through the knowledge resulting
> from meditation,
> By your master's blessings and within your
> mind's composure,
> And is not the pursuit of the shifting intellect.

The dry theory of conceptualizing
Through endless speculations and lists of
     contradictions,
Is in no way equal to seeing the nature of your
     mind.

Well, you may now wonder, "What is the actual view of
seeing your own nature through the traditions of these
profound paths?"

The Middle Way, the unity of the two truths
     beyond limitations,
Mahamudra, the basic wakefulness of the
     uncontrived natural state,
And the Great Perfection, the original
     Samantabhadra of primordial purity—
Are all in agreement on a single identical
     meaning.

This mind that is present in all beings
Is in essence an original emptiness, not made out
     of anything whatsoever.
By nature it is unimpeded experience, aware and
     knowing.
Their unity, unfathomable by the intellect,
Defies such attributes as being present or absent,

existent or nonexistent, permanent or
    nothingness.

Spontaneously present since the beginning, yet
    not created by anyone,
This self-existing and self-manifest natural
    awareness, your basic state,
Has a variety of different names:
In the Prajnaparamita vehicle it is called innate
    truth.
The vehicle of Mantra calls it natural luminosity.
While a sentient being it is named sugata-
    essence.
During the path it is given names which describe
    the view, meditation, and so forth.
And at the point of fruition it is named
    dharmakaya of buddhahood.
All these different names and classifications
Are nothing other than this present ordinary
    mind.

Before being spoiled by delusion it is called
    primordial purity.
When deluded and covered by defilement it is
    named all-ground.

The moment you recognize the falsity of
    delusion is called the view.

To sustain that recognition undistractedly is
    known as meditation.
To be undeluded throughout daily activities is
    named conduct.
When habitual tendencies and delusion are
    purified is called fruition.

Thus this single mind itself
Receives endless names and classifications
Due to the different situations of ground, path
    and fruition.

The eloquent ocean-like words of the buddhas
Are all given solely for the purpose of realizing
    this nature.
Still people are bewildered and confuse
    themselves
With all these names and words.

Being indivisibly knowing, aware and empty,
This mind itself holds no duality of seer and
    seen.
To see this is called realizing the natural state of
    the view.

Setting aside the blessings of the true
    transmission, the element of devotion,
Neither perfecting the accumulations nor
    purifying the obscurations,
Someone endowed with a lucid memory, vast
    learning,

And brilliant scrutiny is still unable to realize
  this nature.
It requires a worthy person with the right karmic
  potential.

The siddha Luhipa said it like this:

You should regard the phenomena of samsara
  and nirvana
Neither as concrete nor abstract, nor as both or
  neither.
That which is hard to point out to a childish
  person results from serving a master,
Once you discover it through him, you will see
  this unseen nature.

In the vajra songs of Tilopa you find this:

This intrinsic and innate wakefulness
Remains at the very heart of all beings.
And yet, it is never perfected without being
  pointed out by a master.

The incomparable Gampopa continues:

Not the domain of the ordinary person,
Nor known by someone of great learning,

It is understood by the devoted,
Depends on the path of blessings,
And is supported by the master's words.

Gyalwa Drigungpa said:

Secret Mantra is the path of blessings.
Unless you receive a master's blessings,
Whatever you realize is constructed by thought.
And thought is taught to be superficial and
    obscuring.
Therefore serve a master
And supplicate him tirelessly.

Thus the way to unmistakenly realize the view, the
nature of the basic state, depends upon devotion and
blessings.

Having thus seen the nature of the view,
How then should one practice?

In the case of the lower vehicles
You are taught to establish the view as emptiness
By analyzing with discriminating knowledge.
The practice is to then train in combining
    emptiness and compassion
And to endeavor in gathering accumulations and
    purifying obscurations.

Commonly, both the outer and inner Secret
    Mantra
Teach you to train, as a unity,
In the development stage of deity yoga
And the completion stage with and without
    attributes
Within the state that is sealed with the view.

It is indeed wonderful that,
Being ingenious at using skillful means,
The buddhas have taught
All these different classifications
To influence disciples with complex inclinations.

However, in this context, the practice of
    Mahamudra and Dzogchen,
The very pinnacle of vehicles,
Is not at all like these other teachings
In which their meditations and the view remain
    disconnected.

Here the view and meditation are not kept
    separate
But are simply an indivisible unity:
The view of seeing your basic state,
Not by fabricating it, but by allowing it to
    resume its natural flow.

According to people's different capacities,
For the highest, the unity of shamatha and
    vipashyana

Is pointed out from the very first.
There is no need to compose the meditation
  state and pursue the post-meditation.
Instead, realization and liberation are
  simultaneous
Within the all-pervasive expanse of your innate
  nature.

For those of you with medium and lesser
  capacities, in common,
Bring forth signs by means of the preliminary
  practices,
And then thoroughly resolve the view.
When you are easily able to see the nature of
  mind,
Maintain the quality of stillness.
Deeply relaxing body, speech and mind,
Don't pursue any thoughts about past or future,
But allow your present wakefulness to look
  directly into itself.

Neither inhibit nor indulge
The six sense impressions of sights, sounds,
  smells, and so forth.
Towards every experience, whatever takes place,
Be awake, lucid, and fresh
While maintaining a balance between being
  collected and relaxed.

When too concentrated, you manufacture a
  state.

When too lax, you diffuse into the undercurrent
    of thought.
Instead, to simply remain undistracted
Is itself the supreme shamatha
Which is taught to be the foundation for
    meditation training.

These days, there seem to be some practitioners
    of shamatha
Who regard the state of nonthought in which
    the six senses are shut down
As the most eminent.
This is called the "serenity of cessation,"
And it is taught to be a flaw and side-track of
    meditation training,
Which only results in a rebirth in either a
    formless realm
Or as a naga or an animal.
Either way, it never leads to liberation.

This indeed is what Lord Sakyapa meant when he said:

It is taught that fools who train in "Mahamudra"
Mainly cause [rebirth as] an animal.
If not, they take rebirth in the formless realms,
Or else they fall into the cessation of a shravaka.

In any case, all sutras and tantras emphasize that enlightenment is never attained through stubbornly training in nonthought by suppressing thought activity. The *Lalita Vistara* phrases it like this:

> When embarking upon true enlightenment,
>   Shakyamuni, the Tathagata,
> Formed the resolve to attain buddhahood
>   through emptiness.
> When at the banks of Nairanjana, he remained
>   in motionless samadhi,
> The conqueror Immutable Sky appeared filling
>   the sky like a full sesame pod.
> Snapping his fingers at the son of the
>   conquerors, he spoke in verse:
> "This meditation state is not the perfect one.
> Through it you will not attain the ultimate.
> Instead bring forth the most eminent
>   wakefulness, as vast as the sky's expanse!"

The story continued:

> When he heard these words he abandoned the
>   motionless samadhi.

Thus it is taught in great detail.

There is also the story about how Nyang Ben Tingdzin Zangpo once received instruction in meditation from a Chinese Hashang teacher. Practicing assiduously, he had many visions including conditioned types of superknowledge. Impressed with his own excellent meditation, he met the great pandita Vimalamitra and said, "Due to my samadhi I can remain immersed for many days without any thought of food or drink." Vimalamitra responded with displeasure, "Through that you will take rebirth as a *naga*. It's useless!" Nyang Ben then began to follow the great pandita, requested the Great Perfection from him and, by practicing it, attained the body of light.

When Lord Gampopa related to Milarepa how he had had excellent samadhi experiences through meditating using the Kadam instructions, Milarepa laughed and said, "You don't get butter from squeezing sand. Instead of that, practice this instruction of mine."

There are many such stories, so apart from the supreme type of shamatha, it is obviously essential that we don't become involved in the inferior types of shamatha or the shamatha of cessation.

Therefore, do not inhibit any experience
Such as the six sense impressions,
And don't stray into fixating or indulging.
If you endeavor in this supreme shamatha
Of resting loosely in the composure of naturalness,
You will have the experiences of movement,
    attainment,
Familiarization, stability and perfection.

It is exceedingly important that
No matter how many superficial, conditioned
    qualities you have—
Such as experiences of bliss, clarity and nonthought,
Superknowledges, visions, miraculous powers,
    and so forth—
You should not get involved in feeling conceited,
Fascinated, attached or proud.
Yet, even so, I have seen many meditators who
    became seduced
By such experiences, visions, and signs on the
    path.

The sugata Phagmo Drubpa said:

Without experiencing lucid wakefulness, free
    from fixation,
One clings to the meditation-moods of bliss and
    clarity.
It is useless to meditate with a conceptual frame
    of mind
Won't it only create a rebirth as a formless god?

He also said:

The person of great power and ability
Ends up performing endless rituals for pay.

The meditator with [attachment to] clear dreams
Invokes enslavement by evil spirits

Milarepa said:

When even evil spirits and non-Buddhists
Possess such common and fleeting qualities,
Without the realization of nonduality
How can these possibly suffice to make you a
    siddha?

Consequently, there is no fault greater than this evil
spirit of ego-clinging.

Therefore, when you become adept in the
    flawless shamatha
You stabilize the foundation for meditation
    training.

The original wakefulness of vipashyana
    belonging to the main part
Depends exclusively on having or not having
Received the blessings and pointing-out
    instruction.
Apart from that, even the thoughts of worldly
    folk
Are indeed vipashyana manifest as conceptual
    thinking.

Even that which sustains the meditation state of
  shamatha
Is nothing other than vipashyana.
That which sees, notices, or feels
Whether there is stillness or movement,
  distraction or no distraction,
Is also the knowing wakefulness of vipashyana.

There is no other vipashyana superior to this
Which needs to be separately accomplished.
Therefore, from the very outset,
The supreme shamatha and vipashyana
Co-exist and are spontaneously present.

For this reason, the vital point that the shamatha of cessation by suppressing sensations is ineffective is due to
the fault that it blocks off vipashyana. The qualities of
realizing the ultimate fruition, all the unique attributes of
buddhahood, the 37 qualities that are aspects of enlightenment, and so forth, as well as the virtues of the twofold supreme knowledge, are all exclusively the outcome
of vipashyana. Consequently, no matter how stable you
become in the shamatha that suppresses vipashyana, you
will not be liberated. That is both the reason and the crucial point.

Whether your mind is still or whether it moves,
Whatever state it happens to be in,
In essence, it is an unidentifiable freshness,
That has neither color, shape, nor attributes.
And yet, its unobstructed knowing is wide awake.

Whatever thought unfolds, whether good or
    evil,
It is an utter openness, made out of nothing
    concrete.
In any of the six sense impressions, whatever is
    experienced,
It is totally insubstantial, with no clinging to
    solidity.

Without sinking into dull mindlessness,
It is utter brilliance, aware and awake.
To recognize the natural face of this ordinary
    mind,
Uncorrupted by the meditation-moods of bliss,
    clarity and emptiness,
Is known as vipashyana, clear seeing.
Unanimously this is the very heart
Of Mahamudra, the Middle Way, Pacifying, and
    Cutting.
So simply recognize that alone!

This is exactly what in all the philosophical vehicles is called the "vipashyana that discerns and fully realizes phenomena, just as they are." Nevertheless, it is rare that someone actually brings it into personal experience rather than feeling it is sufficient to just leave it as only a name or theory.

In the context of emphasizing the "path of means" within the vehicle of Secret Mantra, it is known as "intrinsic wakefulness of empty bliss" and by other such names. In the context of the "path of liberation" such as Mahamudra, Dzogchen, Pacifying, Cutting, and so forth, this type of vipashyana is called the "vipashyana which knows the thatness of mind as it is."

After having finally realized it, at the time of non-meditation of the Mahamudra system or "culmination of awareness," according to Dzogchen, it is called the "vipashyana that realizes the innate nature exactly as it is."

Understand that these three types of vipashyana are all included within simply recognizing the natural face of your present ordinary mind.

I have now described both the flaws and qualities of shamatha, as well as the nature of vipashyana. I have also described how the supreme shamatha and vipashyana are indivisible and how to sustain this unity. Without a doubt this is the description of the main part of meditation.

Nevertheless, in accordance with the general approach of the teachings, I shall now express once more, as a brief hint, how to proceed on a daily basis with the actual practice.

When someone has reached stability in
  shamatha
Or, if not, at least gained some degree of
  certainty,
How do they then continue the daily practice?

The different approaches of the various guidance
  manuals
Teach us to seek the "meditation through the
  view" or the "view through meditation."
As the intent and purpose is the same,
In any of these various systems outlining the
  sequence or order
For "mind-search" and shamatha training that
  you happen to follow,
They are always identical in meditation and
  post-meditation.

The guidance in the view of the Middle Way
Teaches that the meditation state is to train
  exclusively in emptiness,
While in the post-meditation you cultivate
Loving kindness and compassion, like a magical
  illusion.

In that system, the meditation state is called
  "space-like dhyana"
And the post-meditation "magical samadhi."

About this, Lord Gampopa said:

> The followers of the Paramita vehicle train in meditation after establishing, by means of scriptures and reasoning, that dependent origination and so forth are experienced while being devoid of a self-nature. Thus they create emptiness out of devoted interest. This is the meditation system of the Middle Way which means there is a dualistic attitude involved in holding the notions of meditator and meditation object. Through this you don't realize the view. Because of counteracting the fixation on concreteness, it can purify boundless obscurations, but it cannot bring enlightenment.

He continued:

> Others briefly place themselves in the meditation on complete nonthought and train in the post-meditation as being dream and magical illusion. In the system of Guru Milarepa, you train in the five poisons and in every thought being nondual wakefulness. Once adept, you train in nothing but the meditation state beyond sessions and breaks.

Thus he taught in great detail.

In all Mahamudra systems, the beginning yogis
Make the meditation state the main part of the
    sessions
While the post-meditation is to sustain it with
    mindfulness during the activities of the
    breaks.
Once they have realized some degree of
    familiarization,
It is taught that everything then becomes purely
    the meditation state.

Dzogchen systems, for the most part,
Being intended for the instantaneous type of
    person,
Teach while condensing everything into the
    dividing point between knowing and not
    knowing,
Rather than dividing between meditation and
    post-meditation.

Whichever is the case, the crucial point in the
    practice
Is not to get involved in deliberately projecting
    or concentrating
Upon the state of your present naked mind,
But rather, simply to recognize your nature in
    whatever you experience, no matter what
    it is.
That which sustains this is given the name
    "mindfulness."

Although in shamatha an emphasis on stillness is
    taught,
At this point you bring everything into the
    training, be it stillness or thinking.

Whether your thoughts manifest as "evil,"
Such as the five poisonous emotions, pain, and
    sickness,
Or in the various forms of goodness,
Such as devotion and compassion, renunciation
    and pure perception,
Whatever you experience, realize that all of it
Is simply the unobstructed play of your own
    mind.
Without rejecting with anger or accepting with
    attachment,
Rest loosely in the innate state of same taste.

Let go into your natural state, with no need to
    cling to or fixate on
Even the impetus or the attitude "I meditate!"
Without disturbing yourself with any ambition,
Such as hoping for a good meditation or fearing
    it won't succeed,
To let be in unfabricated naturalness free from
    concepts,
Is the meditation state of all the systems of
    definitive meaning.

It is deluded fixation to cling to solid reality
While you walk, sit, eat, lie down or talk.
But when you never separate yourself from the
    training during any daily activity,
Simply recognizing your nature, while remaining
    undistracted,
Is still the meditation state itself, even though it
    may be called "post-meditation."

Unless you know how to sustain the natural
    mode of your innate nature,
You may keep the posture and gaze, but it still
    isn't meditation.
In short, as long as you embrace whatever you
    experience with a sense of wakefulness,
All you do is meditation training.
But if not, though your stillness may be steady, it
    is only a blocked state of indifference.
Therefore, simply sustain the recognition of
    ordinary mind.

In the *Sutra on Pure Intention* you find this passage:

Manjushri asked, "What is a meditating monk's
experience of samadhi?"

The [Buddha] replied, "It is like the smoke from a
chimney ceasing when the flames in the fireplace are
extinguished. Once he understands and sees that mind

is empty, he will have the experience that visual forms are empty appearance, sounds are empty resounding, smells are empty sensation, flavors are empty tasting, and textures are empty feeling. Thus, the sky clears when not obscured; water clears when not stirred up; and mind eases when not contrived."

He continued:

> The monk who knows the nature of mind
> Continues the meditation training, no matter
>   what he does;
> He remains in the innate nature.

If you can abide by sustaining what he taught, you will have no great difficulty in maintaining a continuous meditation state.

Furthermore, you don't need to suppress thought movement, the six sense impressions and so forth, as the Dzogchen scriptures mention:

> When the mind's fixating thought
> Does not engage in the lucid cognitions of the
>   five senses,
> This itself is the buddha mind.

You also find this quotation:

> The pleasures and painful states you have in
>   dreams

Are all of an equal nature the moment you
    wake up.
Likewise, the states of thought and nonthought
Are of equal nature in the moment of awareness.

In the *Dzogchen Hearing Lineage of Aro* you find this:

Like the analogy of a cloud in the sky,
While your mind creates projections
They appear but don't harm its basic ground.
Similarly, within the awakened state of mind,
Thoughts don't obscure and need not be
    corrected.

The Golden Garland of Rulu mentions:

The yogi who realizes this
Will rest his mind in unfabricated freshness;
So don't block off your senses but rest them in
    their natural state.
Sight, sound, smell, taste and texture—
In whatever you see and whatever you experience,
Compose yourself freely in the state of simply
    that.
Without inhibiting and without holding on,
Remain in equanimity, the state of awareness.

There are innumerable similar quotations. Since all
the 6,400,000 tantras of the Great Perfection unani-

mously teach this very same crucial point, why should I keep citing more quotes? Similarly, all the scriptures on Mahamudra have nothing other than this same basic intent. This is why the glorious Shavaripa said:

> Cutting to its root, mind is like the sky.
> It is not some "thing" to be cultivated, so don't
>   mentally form it.
> Just like space cannot observe space,
> Likewise emptiness cannot imagine emptiness.

He also sang:

> In this way, at any moment throughout the three
>   times,
> To simply sustain the boundless innate state of
>   nondoing mind,
> Is given the name "meditation."
> Don't control the breath, don't tie down
>   thought,
> But rest your mind uncontrived, like a small
>   child.
>
> When starting to think, look into that itself.
> Don't conceive of the wave being different from
>   the water.
> Within the Mahamudra of nondoing mind,
> There is not even a speck of dust to be meditated
>   forth, so don't create something by
>   meditating.

The supreme meditation is to never depart from
the nature of nonmeditation.

The glorious Naropa said:

When looking, look into your own mind.
Since this mind is not made out of anything,
Indescribable, and beyond any object,
It is unconstructed, like the sky.

Lord Marpa sang:

In general, no matter how the perceived is seen,
When not realized, it is a deluded perception
And tied down by clinging to outer objects.
For the realized, it is seen as a magical illusion,
So perceived objects dawn as helpers.
In the ultimate sense there is never any
     perception;
It is utterly freed into nonarising dharmakaya.

Within, this consciousness of moving thoughts,
When not realized, is ignorance,
The basis for karma and disturbing emotions.
When realized, it is a self-knowing wakefulness,
Which perfects all virtuous qualities.
In the ultimate sense, since all phenomena are
     brought to exhaustion,
It is taught that original wakefulness doesn't
     really exist.

The conqueror Götsangpa said:

> Look directly into your own mind.
> When looking it is unseen and inconcrete.
> Rest loosely in this absence.
> Remain free and easy, without fixation.
>
> When once again a thought begins to move,
> Recognize its nature directly,
> And rest loosely in simply that.
> Beyond a doubt, it dissolves into itself.

The siddha Orgyenpa sang:

> During the experience of ordinary mind,
> While practicing, undistracted like the continuos
>   flow of a river,
> Let loose your mind,
> Unbridled and without any fabrication be utterly
>   free.

To summarize, all the scriptures and instructions of Mahamudra and Dzogchen, as well as all the oral advice of the lineage masters, exclusively teach how to continue the training with no difference between stillness and thought occurrence. Likewise, they also describe nothing other than how to use sense perceptions, thoughts and so on, as helpers without rejecting them.

Although this is so, I see that nowadays there are still a predominant number of meditators, of both the New and

Old schools, who understand the word "nondistraction" to mean that meditation is to sustain a state of stillness and that everything else is not meditation training. After this, they set their minds on nothing but shamatha.

Therefore, I feel that not only are we at a time when the Vinaya teachings and the practice of the general tradition of Secret Mantra, for the most part, are being distorted and are in decline, but even the teachings of the Practice Lineage are close to fading away.

This basic state of originally pure natural
    awareness
Is unseen by oneself, like the treasure in a poor
    man's house.
Once you realize it through the guru's kindness,
You personally know the indivisible three kayas
    to be your own nature.

At that moment, the view, meditation, conduct
    and fruition, the paths, bhumis and so on,
All these many classifications with delectable
    names,
By resolving their root, the heart of the matter,
You cut through the hope of success and the fear
    of failure.

If you begin to desire the gifts of experiences and
    insights, signs and indications of progress,

You are already possessed by attachment and
    ego-clinging,
And there will never be a chance for meditation
    training.

While the qualities of samsara and nirvana are
    spontaneously present in the ground,
Failing to acknowledge this, to hanker after the
    signs of the path as well as a result,
Is far inferior to even the Hinayana.
All side-tracks, obscurations, and obstacles arise
    from this.

A person who understands that samsara and
    nirvana are both mind,
Is free from the basis for any occurrence
Of side-tracks, deviations, and mistakes,
And will therefore possess the qualities of
    fruition, effortlessly and spontaneously.

Tilopa described it in these words:

When you realize the equal nature
Of these three: view, meditation and conduct,
There is no duality of good and evil.
But if you hold some other thought,
You have no confidence and are deluded.

Gampopa also said:

> For the view, free from change,
> Have a realization that cuts through ground and
> root.
> For the meditation, free from sessions and breaks,
> Remain continuously throughout the three times.
>
> For the conduct, free from hypocrisy,
> Possess an altruism that is not self-seeking.
> For the fruition, free from hope and fear,
> Bring your training to perfection.

The shortcoming of expecting to quickly have signs of progress or experience and realization and other qualities, without having cut through the ego-oriented frame of mind, is described by the accomplished master Lingje Repa:

> If you wish to see the buddha mind,
> Hankering after signs of progress only postpones
> it.
> Once your wishing for signs of progress is
> exhausted,
> You have arrived at the buddha mind.

He also said:

> As long as you retain conceptual clinging,
> You will never cross the river of samsara.

To let go of fixation is the key point of liberation;
When free from subtle attachment, you are a
    buddha.

Now, in accordance with the subject about which
    you inquire,
To describe the crucial points of and the dividing
    line between
Whether or not genuine realization has taken
    place,
Since I have previously often written about
The four yogas of Mahamudra and the four
    visions of Dzogchen, and so forth,
I shall not enumerate them again here.
Nevertheless, as the very heart of this matter,
I will explain the following in order to make the
    distinction
Between these two: experience and realization.

In the general vehicles including the Middle
    Way
The stages are described with many names, such
    as the thirty-seven aspects of enlightenment
Corresponding to the force of training in the
    samadhi of emptiness and compassion,
So I cannot explain them all here.
You can look for them in the major scriptures.

In any case, since all the categories of qualities
    belonging to gradual progress
On the paths and stages of the general vehicles
Are complete within this swift path,
And since you don't need to depend on such
    words if you accomplish it's nature,
I will set aside such elaborations.

In this system, during the four yogas and so forth,
To gain confidence in the indivisible unity
Of the essence of the training and your mind,
Is called the "dawn of realization" and is itself
    enough.

Until that happens, as long as you maintain that
    the practice in which you train
Is separate from mind, the meditator,
Or that the sustainer of mindfulness is different
    from the object sustained,
You have still not glimpsed the heart of
    realization.

Therefore bliss, clarity or nonthought,
No matter what occurs—all these meditation-
    moods and experiences—
Are nothing but the outer "peels" of the
    meditation training,
So they are never to be fondly clung to.

The uninterrupted experience of greater one-
    pointedness,

The simplicity of everything dawning as
    emptiness, and so forth
Are all nothing but meditation-moods and
    experiences—so give up conceit!

The meditator and the meditation object are the
    mind itself.
Distraction and mindfulness are both mind as
    well.
Good thoughts and bad thoughts are all the
    mind itself.
Recognizing the natural face is also this mind
    itself.

Once you resolve that everything is solely your
    own mind,
It is easy to realize the view of indivisible
    samsara and nirvana.
Once you resolve the root and basis of the view
    within yourself,
There is no meditation object apart from this
    single awareness.
Since it is never separate from you throughout
    the three times,
It is indeed not hard to have realization.

Nevertheless, the meditator who isn't resolved
    about mind,
Though meditating for a hundred aeons, will
    still cling to the meditation-moods.

Due to this clinging, which is the sole root cause
    of samsara,
There is no way to realize the fruition of
    Mahamudra or Dzogchen.

All classifications and dividing points are
    included within this.

True realization is when you are free from the
    peels of the meditation-moods.
Though named "realization," it is uncorrupted
    awareness itself.
This uncorrupted awareness, your natural state,
Is itself the single aim of practice.

Because of different capacities, higher, medium
    and lesser
There can be rapid realization, gradual
    realization, and so forth.
But if you simply continue training until
    perfection,
You will be liberated into the primordial ground
    of the "exhaustion of phenomena and
    concepts."

Just like someone who has recovered from an
    epidemic,
You have no fear of again being deluded into
    samsara.

Having perfected the kayas and wisdoms, as well
    as the training,
An effortless compassion will spontaneously
    accomplish the welfare of beings.

Condensed to the essence, this ordinary mind,
Should be left as it naturally is and nothing else.
Striving for an eminent view and meditation,
    training in artifice,
Desiring experiences and realization, and to progress
    through the paths and stages of the yogas
While fearing going astray or taking sidetracks,
    and so forth,
Totally abandon all such pursuits.

Lord Götsangpa said, "To condense everything into
one point, I will simply practice this unimpaired present
ordinary mind until reaching the state of buddhahood."
Besides following this statement of his, don't harbor
ambitions about anything else whatsoever.

    The supreme being and lord of the Dharma (Chöje
Rinpoche) said:

    Some accept that when the steadiness of the
        meditation state
    Has become continuous with
    The unbroken lucid wakefulness during post-
        meditation,

Is itself the realization of the buddha-mind.

This is exactly what I too have understood:
That the nakedness of ordinary mind is the
    dharmakaya
In which both meditation and post-meditation,
    along with habitual tendencies,
Are forever vanquished, like iron filed totally
    away.

He continued:

    While striving for qualities, you get stuck in the
        viscous disease of ambition.
    While trying to acquire a fruition, it is destroyed
        by the frost of expectations.
    While wishing for signs of progress, you get
        caught in the trap of Mara.

It is just as he has taught.

    Though numerous types of conduct for
        enhancement are taught,
    Including equal taste and yogic disciplines,
    When you simply tame your own stream-of-
        being
    You have no need for any other equal taste.

These days, all practitioners claim,
"I'm a meditator!, I'm a yogi!, I'm a mendicant!"
While chasing donations given out of faith.
They may wear the right costumes,
But when meeting the slightest disrespect, given
  measly offerings
Or hearing even the smallest criticism,
They forget their meditation and spiritual
  practice,
And, like a viper, fly into a rage.
How can there be any progress in their spiritual
  practice?
For such people, what is the use of equal taste?

Therefore it is not at all necessary
To live in scary solitudes
Or to engage in the yogic disciplines of pursuing
  confrontations;
Rather, it is most eminent, though very rare,
To exclusively live by the key point
Of a spiritual practice that transcends the eight
  worldly concerns.

Once a meditator from the Drigung school who claimed
to have perfected the practice of illusory body was told
by Kyobpa Rinpoche, "People say you have broken your
vows; that is extremely offensive." When he got furious,

Kyobpa Rinpoche said, "Since you claimed to have perfected the illusory body, I was testing you." The story goes that through this his pride was reduced.

Gyalsey Togmey Rinpoche also said:

> When my belly is full and the sun shines, I look
>   like a practitioner.
> When confronting adversity I am an ordinary
>   person.
> Since my mind has not mingled with the
>   Dharma,
> Grant your blessings that my heart may be
>   flexible.

As he said, this is obviously something to revere a hundred times at the crown of your head.

Furthermore, unless the Dharma tames your mind, there is no benefit in merely wearing the attire of a yogi or a monk. The *Udana Varga* mentions:

> The Blessed One addressed the monks, "How can the shaving of a monk's head possibly be enlightenment? How can yellow robes possibly be enlightenment? How can rinsing oneself with water possibly

be enlightenment? How can refraining from taking meals after noon possibly be enlightenment?"

His followers grew doubtful and uncertain and then said, "That being so, through what does one attain enlightenment?"

The Buddha replied, "Shave the hair of conceptual thinking with the razor of discriminating knowledge. Protect yourself from the aches of disturbing emotions with the robes of emptiness. Rinse away your ignorance with the water of wisdom. Dispel the hunger of desire with the food of meditation."

Here is how the awakened state is never attained simply through vast learning or extensive understanding unless one's mind is mingled with the Dharma. To quote, the *Sutra of Nonorigination of Dharmas* says:

> Correct behavior and the rectification of
> mistakes,
> Fondness of words and talk—none of these
> indicate purity.
> Unless you fully comprehend the nature of the
> truth,
> You don't awaken to enlightenment through
> exactness in words.

The Buddha Avatamsaka Sutra mentions:

> The true teachings of the Buddha
> Are not accomplished through learning alone.
> While forcibly carried away by a river
> Feeble people may still die of thirst.
> The teaching you fail to practice is similar to
> this.

The same text continues:

> The steersman of a boat or ship
> On a river or on the ocean
> Though able to ferry others across,
> May still die on the water himself.
> The teaching you fail to practice is similar to
> this.

In this way it is has been taught in numerous other texts.

Most people, including myself, who nowadays claim to be practitioners, are nothing but what the conqueror Yang-gönpa describes in his *Advice*:

> All of us who follow the side of Dharma, unable
> to practice during even a single night's sleep, dur-

ing the actions of even a single day or even during a short activity, occupy ourselves exclusively with achievements for this life. When we feel like practicing the sacred Dharma, we do it; when we don't feel like it, we suspend it. Sometimes, when it is convenient, we do it; when not, we suspend it.

We wish to meditate without spending time learning how. We wish to have signs of accomplishment without spending time in meditation training. With no time to practice the Dharma, we wish to immediately be a siddha or a *tokden*, to have superknowledges and miraculous powers or to be something extraordinary.

When this doesn't happen, we interrupt our Dharma practice, discouraging ourselves by thinking, "Someone like me cannot possibly have success in practice." We all want to be enlightened without meditating or practicing, but it just won't happen!

He also said:

We need to take up a diligent course of action and practice throughout day and night. We may pretend to be someone who lives in a mountain hermitage and does retreat. We may feign being a good meditator, while chatting all day and sleeping all night. When we come out of retreat and go down from the mountain hermitage, we have neither progressed nor advanced in our spiritual practice. In mind and character we are still totally rigid and uptight. To be a Dharma practitioner in appearance only won't help at all.

He said as well:

> You may have met with a master who is like the Buddha in person, received the nectar-like oral instructions and possess a meditation that is like Kailash, the king of snow mountains. Still, you won't be enlightened unless you also tame your mind. The meditator surely needs to have experiences and realization. Yet apart from meditating, no one will come along to give them to him.

He gave lots of similar advice all of which is only too true.

Once again, unless you can chiefly practice the very heart of the Dharma, it will be difficult to find something else that brings accomplishment. The *Sutra of the Good Aeon* states:

> Besides abiding in the true practice,
> You will not attain supreme enlightenment by
> any other means.

As just said, if you can focus on practicing the profound key points of oral instruction, you effectively use the essence of all the teachings in full. The *Sutra of the King of Samadhi* describes this:

> Whichever sutra I have taught
> In all the world systems,
> The words have but a single meaning.
> You cannot practice all of them,
> But by practicing just a single sentence,
> You will be practicing them all.

It is exactly as the Buddha just said. This being so, it is not necessary to immediately have visible signs of special traits or good qualities, but rather, to accomplish all true needs and thereby attain what is of lasting value. The Precious Master of Uddiyana said:

> Empty awareness can in no way be harmed by external things nor can any adversity obstruct it. By resolving the nature of samsara, you won't find any basis for taking rebirth among the six classes of beings. By capturing the fabric of thought within the nature of instantaneous awareness, the evil zombie of disturbing emotions cannot possibly rise up again within unconditioned empty knowing. By bringing the roots of karmic ripening to exhaustion, misdeeds are swept away. By being free from re-occurrence of body and speech, the inroads to

the lower realms are blocked. By recognizing all that appears and exists to be mind, the hells are utterly nonexistent. When meeting with such oral instructions, the person who practices unwaveringly and one-pointedly doesn't need to fear death, since within this life he has already accomplished the task of lasting value.

For this to happen you need to exert yourself.

Therefore, all of you who intend to make use of
  these freedoms and riches,
Follow a sublime spiritual teacher and resolve
  uncertainty about the instructions.
Reflect sincerely upon your mortality and cast
  away attachment to this world.
Equalize the eight worldly concerns and mingle
  your minds with the Dharma.

As the essence of view and meditation, sustain
  naked awareness.
As the essence of daily activities, follow the
  example of the masters of the Practice
  Lineage.
As the essence of precepts and samayas, don't
  belittle the law of cause and effect.
As the essence of activity, subdue the evil spirit
  of selfishness.

Don't stray into nihilistic dissipation; bring the
teachings into actual practice.
Don't pursue details with attachment; realize
everything to be like a magical illusion.
Don't bind yourself in the chains of duality; be
carefree and unfettered.
It is extremely important to understand the key
points of the Dharma.

Alas! In this dark age when all afflictions
coincide,
And the chariot of the Buddha's teachings sinks
into the muddy swamp,
No matter how much you intend to work for the
benefit of the teachings,
It is hopeless to expect it to truly help the
Buddhadharma.

The sectarianism of upholding your personal
philosophical view,
The business of maintaining a monastery and
keeping followers,
The devices for acquiring the necessities of
funds and food,
Cause nothing but personal regret and others'
scorn.

Meaningless words and worldly learning,
Volumes of information, and the pretentious
aims of fame and material gain,

Maintaining the artificial guise of a master which
    ruins both self and others,
I make the wish to never again pursue any of
    these.

In forests and unpeopled valleys, as praised by
    the Buddha,
With the renunciation of knowing that nothing
    is needed,
May I and all others without exception exert
    ourselves
In facing the original buddha of our own minds.

By the power of the virtue of writing down, with
    pure motivation,
The vital points for embarking on the essential
    view and meditation of all the teachings
Supported by the statements spoken by the
    victorious ones,
May the ocean of samsara quickly dry up and
    may all beings attain enlightenment!

Though I have written this in response to a request from
the monk Mönlam who expressed the need for such notes
on the key points for practicing the view and meditation of the profound path of Mahamudra, Dzogchen,
and Madhyamika, I personally possess neither definitive
experience nor realization, so this will hardly be in accor-

dance with their exact meaning. All I have expressed here may be nothing more than nonsense, like the babbling of someone drunk on wine. Nevertheless, I wrote this with the single pure intention of benefiting others, free from any extraneous defilements.

So as to be easily understood by everyone, both high and low, and avoiding the flowery words of poetics, I have emphasized straightforward meaning in ordinary language. In this cliff-overhang hermitage of Götsangpa's cave, I, Natsok Rangdröl, wrote this at the auspicious event of the first day of the waxing part of the second month. Through the outcome of this virtue may all beings reach perfection in their endeavors on a profound path such as this. May it be virtuous!

A small song of realization

> When the guru's and my mind mingled,
>   undivided,
> No longer had my yearning prayer a subject or
>   an object.
> Through this blessing—the knowing of the
>   nature of my mind—
> I received the greatest kindness, most sublime.
>
> Directly looking through the nature of whatever
>   can be known,
> I found no essence of a separate knower.

The looker and looked at, not divided into two:
I found this pointing-out the deepest and the
    most sublime.

Focusing with effort just increases further
    thinking.
A training full of judgments brings no progress.
Keep undistracted and be free of meditating:
This I found to be the greatest key advice.

These words spontaneous were written, as they
    floated to the surface,
In this tramp, a Dharmaless and aimless drifter.
May they help the unfree beings to transcend
    their every anguish
And reach simplicity, the ultimate attainment.

These were written while in retreat when I (Tsele
Natsok Rangdröl) was twenty-three years old.

Translator's Afterword

Lamp of Mahamudra is the second of three renowned books by Tsele Natsok Rangdröl and was translated at the command of Dilgo Khyentse Rinpoche, and the kind encouragement and teachings of Tulku Urgyen Rinpoche and Chökyi Nyima Rinpoche. I completed the first edition at Nagi Gompa in 1987. Still later, Zack Beer reviewed the text with the edition published by Shambhala and rechecked it against the Tibetan for this new presentation, in 2007. Thanks go to him and Marcia Binder Schmidt for acting as the translation and production assistant, checking all stages of the work, Judith Amtzis for her repeated editing, as well as John Rockwell, Thomas Doctor and Wayne Amtzis for their useful suggestions.

According to the command, encouragement and teachings of my lords of refuge Tulku Urgyen and Chökyi Nyima Rinpoches, I made the first inadequate rendering of *Heart of the Matter* also at Nagi Gompa. Through their continuing kind guidance an additional feeble attempt a translation was made at Pal Rangjung Yeshe Gomde in Denmark and completed at Nagi Gompa in Nepal in 1997. At that time, it was finalized with the help of Khenpo Chadrel and Lama Putsi Pema Tashi. The text was compared with the Tibetan by Marcia Binder

Schmidt, and edited by Michael Tweed and S. Lhamo did proofreading.

These texts both were translated for use at the yearly seminar conducted by Rangjung Yeshe Institute at Pal Ka-Nying Shedrub Ling Monastery, Boudhanath, Kathmandu, Nepal.

Tsele Natsok Rangdröl is also the author of *Mirror of Mindfulness, Empowerment*, and *Circle of the Sun*.

By the power of the aspirations of Tsele Natsok Rangdröl, may this book be a direct cause of furthering the practice of the Buddha's teachings and of bringing benefit to countless beings.

Erik Pema Kunsang
Rangjung Yeshe Gomde, Denmark, 2009

WELL-WISHES

NAMO GURU BUDDHA BODHISATVAYA
Extracted meaning of the Jina's spoken words
    and all the shastras,
The view and training, conduct and fruition
Of Mahamudra, Great Perfection, Middle Way
    and all the rest—
Reconciled without a single contradiction,
Lucid and with key points all complete—
Is this Dharma-relic, so magnificent, a wish-
    fulfilling gem,
Which our perfect teachers, like a living
    Vajradhara,
Bestowed on me and other Vajrayana students.

Through their blessings and symbolic indications,
Through empowerments, their guidance and
    instructions,
May we recognize the nature of our minds
The ultimate and pristine wakefulness.

May we then bring forth experiences and
    realization
In the ten bhumis and the fivefold path,
The twelve aspects of the fourfold yogas,
The fourfold visions and the others states.

I wish that we turn into guides along the
    splendid route to freedom
Like ferrymen who use the sixfold paramitas
And the fourfold magnetizing means
To lead the countless mother-beings from
    samsara's sea.

Whoever makes a wish or supplication just like
    this
May they swiftly too become a true practitioner.

The tulku with the name of Chökyi Nyima composed these lines of well-wishing for a new edition in response to a request from several people whose eyes of Dharma have widely opened.

GLOSSARY FOR
Lamp of Mahamudra

Acceptance (bzod pa). One of the four aspects of ascertainment on the path of joining.

Acharya Shantipa (slob dpon shan ti pa). An Indian master in the Mahamudra lineage.

Aggregate (phung po). *See* "five skandhas."

Akanishtha ('og min). The "highest;" the realm of Vajradhara, the dharmakaya buddha. There are various types of Akanishtha.

Alaya (kun gzhi). The basis of all of samsara and nirvana. *See* "all-ground."

All-encompassing purity (dag pa rab 'byams). The skandhas, elements and so forth of the world and beings, are, in their pure aspects, the five male and female buddhas.

All-ground (kun gzhi, alaya). The basis of mind and both pure and impure phenomena. This word has different meanings in different contexts and should be understood accordingly. Literally it means the "foundation of all things."

All-ground consciousness (kun gzhi'i rnam par shes pa). The cognizant aspect of the "all-ground," like the brightness of a mirror.

All-ground of various tendencies (bag chags sna tshogs pa'i kun gzhi). The alaya serving as the basis for samsaric tendencies.

Appearance and existence (snang srid). Whatever can be experienced [the five elements] and has a possibility of existence [the five aggregates]. This term usually refers to the world and sentient beings.

Attribute (mtshan ma).

Authoritative scriptures (gzhung). Books on philosophy with established validity.

Avatamsaka Sutra (mdo phal po che). A sutra belonging to the third turning of the Wheel of Dharma. Published as *Flower Adornment Sutra*, Shambhala Publications.

Avichi hell (mnar med kyi dmyal ba). The lowest of the eight hot hells.

Awareness discipline (rig pa rtul zhugs). Action free from accepting and rejecting.

Basic straying from the essence of emptiness (stong nyid gshis shor).

Basic straying from the path (lam gyi gshis shor).

Basic straying from the remedy (gnyen po gshis shor).

Basic straying into generalized emptiness (stong nyid rgyas 'debs su gshis shor).

Bhumi (sa). The levels or stages of the bodhisattvas; the ten stages of the last three of the five bodhisattva paths. *See* "ten bhumis."

Bodhichitta (byang sems, byang chub kyi sems). The aspiration to attain enlightenment for the sake of all beings.

Brahmin (bram ze). A person belonging to the priestly caste.

Brilliant ('od 'phro ba). The fourth of the ten bodhisattva bhumis.

Buddha of your own mind (rang sems sangs rgyas). The enlightened essence of one's own mind.

Buddhahood (sangs rgyas). The perfect and complete enlightenment of dwelling in neither samsara nor nirvana.

Causal vehicles (rgyu'i theg pa). Same as the two vehicles, Hinayana and Mahayana. The practitioners of these vehicles regard the practices as the cause for attaining fruition.

Channel, wind, and essence (rtsa rlung thig le). The channels, energies or winds, and essences of the physical body.

Chö (gcod). Pronounced "choe". Literally "cutting." A system of practices based on Prajnaparamita and set down by Machik Labdron for the purpose of cutting through the four Maras and ego-clinging. One of the Eight Practice Lineages of Buddhism in Tibet.

Chökyi Nyima Rinpoche (chos kyi nyi ma rin po che). The abbot of Ka-Nying Shedrub Ling Monastery and the oldest son of Tulku Urgyen Rinpoche. Author of *Union of Mahamudra and Dzogchen* and *Present Fresh wakefulness*, Rangjung Yeshe Publications, 1987.

Chittamatra (sems tsam pa). The Mind Only School of Mahayana, asserting the view that all phenomena are "only" the appearances of "mind."

Cloud of Dharma (chos kyi sprin). The tenth of the ten bodhisattva levels.

Coemergent (lhan cig skyes pa). The two aspects of mind, appearance and emptiness, co-exist. As is said: "Coemergent mind is dharmakaya, coemergent appearance is the light of dharmakaya."

Coemergent ignorance (lhan cig skyes pa'i ma rig pa). "Coemergent" means arising together with or coexisting with one's mind, like sandalwood and its fragrance. "Ignorance" here means lack of knowledge of the nature of mind; in Mahamudra practice the deluded aspect, the moment of oblivion that allows confused thinking to occur.

Coemergent wisdom (lhan cig skyes pa'i ye shes). The innate wakefulness potentially present in all sentient beings. "Wisdom" here means the "primordially undeluded wakefulness."

Cognizant quality (gsal cha). The mind's inherent capacity for knowing.

Common vehicles (thun mong gi theg pa). A term for Hinayana and Mahayana taken together and compared with the "supreme vehicle," Vajrayana.

Complete enlightenment (rdzogs pa'i byang chub). Same as "buddhahood."

Completion stage (rdzogs rim). "Completion stage with marks" is the Six Doctrines. "Completion stage without marks" is the practice of Essence Mahamudra. *See also* "development and completion."

Concept and discernment (rtog dpyod). Gross conception and fine discrimination.

Conceptual ignorance (kun tu brtags pa'i ma rig pa). In Vajrayana, the ignorance of conceptualizing subject and object. In the Sutra system, superimposed or "learned" wrong views. Specifically, in Mahamudra practice it means conceptual thinking.

Confusion and liberation ('khrul grol). Same as samsara and nirvana.

Consciousnesses of the five senses (sgo lnga'i rnam par shes pa). The acts cognizing visual form, sound, smell, taste, and texture.

Cutting through (khregs chod). Cutting through the stream of the thoughts of the three times. Same as "trekcho."

Dakpo Kagyu (dvags po bka' brgyud). The Kagyu lineage as transmitted through Gampopa who is also known as Dakpo Lhaje, the "Doctor from Dakpo."

Defiled mind (nyon yid, nyon mongs pa'i yid kyi rnam par shes pa). The aspect of mind which, taking the all-ground as reference, conceives the thought "I am," one of the eight collections of consciousnesses.

Definitive meaning (nges pa'i don). The direct teachings on emptiness and luminosity as opposed to the expedient meaning, which leads to the definitive meaning.

Dependent (gzhan dbang). One of the "three natures" according to the Chittamatra and Yogachara Schools of philosophy.

Dependent origination (rten cing 'brel bar 'byung ba). The natural law that all phenomena arise "dependent upon" their own causes "in connection with" their individual conditions. The fact that no phenomena appear without a cause and none are made by an uncaused creator, but all arise exclusively due to the coincidence of causes and conditions.

Desire Realm ('dod khams). Comprised of the abodes of hell beings, hungry ghosts, animals, humans, asuras, and the gods of the six abodes of Desire gods, it is called "desire realm" because of the tormented by mental pain caused by gross desire and attachment.

Desire, Form and Formlessness, the realms of ('dod gzugs gzugs med kyi khams). The three realms of samsaric existence.

Development and completion (bskyed rdzogs). The two main aspects of Vajrayana practice. Development stage is fabricated by mind. Completion stage means resting in the unfabricated nature of mind. *See* each individually.

Development stage (bskyed rim, utpattikrama). One of the two aspects of Vajrayana practice which is to create pure images mentally in order to purify habitual tendencies. *See* "development and completion."

Dharma (chos). "Dharma" is the Buddha's teachings; "dharma" means phenomena or mental objects.

Dharma sections (chos kyi phung po). Entities of different teachings such as the 84,000 sections of the Buddha's Words.

Dharma-doors (chos kyi sgo). Figurative expression for the teachings of the buddhas.

Dharmadhatu (chos kyi dbyings). The "realm of phenomena;" the suchness in which emptiness and dependent origination are inseparable. In this context "Dharma" means the truth and "dhatu" means space free from center or periphery. Another explanation is "the nature of phenomena" beyond arising, dwelling and ceasing.

Dharmadhatu palace of Akanishtha ('og min chos kyi dbyings kyi pho brang). Figurative expression for the abode of Vajradhara, the dharmakaya buddha.

Dharmakaya (chos sku). The first of the three kayas, which is devoid of constructs, like space. The nature of all phenomena designated as "body." Should be understood individually according to ground, path and fruition.

Dharmakaya of self-knowing (rang rig chos sku). The dharmakaya aspect of one's own mind.

Dharmakaya Throne of Nonmeditation (bsgom med chos sku'i rgyal sa). The last stage in the yoga of Nonmeditation, which is the complete collapse of fixation and conceptual mind, like a cloud free from the clouds of intellectual meditation. Same as complete and perfect enlightenment.

Dharmata (chos nyid). The nature of phenomena and mind.

Dhyana (bsam gtan). The state of concentrated mind with fixation and also the god realms produced through such mental concentration.

Disturbing emotions (nyon mongs pa). The five poisons of desire, anger, delusion, pride, and envy which tire, disturb, and torment one's mind.

Dohakosha (do ha mdzod). A collection of spontaneous vajra songs by the Indian masters of the Mahamudra lineage.

Drukpa Kagyu school ('brug pa bka' brgyud). The Kagyu teachings transmitted from Gampopa to Phagmo Drubpa.

Dualistic phenomena (gnyis snang). Experience structured as "perceiver" and "object perceived."

Dzogchen (rdzogs pa chen po; rdzogs chen). The teachings beyond the vehicles of causation, first taught in the human world by the great vidyadhara Garab Dorje.

Dzogchen of the Natural State (gnas lugs rdzogs pa chen po). Same as "trekcho," the view of Cutting Through and identical to "Essence Mahamudra."

Eight collections of consciousnesses (rnam shes tshogs brgyad). The all-ground consciousness, mind-consciousness, defiled mind-consciousness, and the five sense-consciousnesses.

Eight deviations (shor sa brgyad). The four basic and the four temporary strayings.

Eight Practice Lineages (sgrub brgyud shing rta brgyad). The eight independent schools of Buddhism that flourished in Tibet: Nyingma, Kadampa, Marpa Kagyu, Shangpa Kagyu, Sakya, Jordruk, Zhije, and Chö.

Eight qualities of mastery (dbang phyug brgyad).

Eight worldly concerns ('jig rten chos brgyad). Attachment to gain, pleasure, praise and fame, and aversion to loss, pain, blame and bad reputation.

Eightfold noble path ('phags lam gyi yan lag brgyad). Literally the "eight aspects of the path of noble beings:" right view, thought, speech, action, livelihood, effort, mindfulness, concentration. These are perfected on the path of cultivation.

Eighty inherent thought states (rang bzhin brgyad cu'i rtog pa). 33 resulting from anger, 40 from desire and 7 from delusion. First, the thirty-three thought states resulting from anger, according to the *Spyod bsDus* composed by Aryadeva, are: detachment, medium detachment, intense detachment, inner mental going, and coming, sadness, medium sadness, intense sadness, quietude, conceptualization, fear, medium fear, intense fear, craving, medium craving, intense craving, grasping, nonvirtue, hunger, thirst, sensation, medium sensation, intense sensation, cognizing, cognizance, perception-basis, discrimination, conscience, compassion, love, medium love, intense love, apprehensiveness, attraction, and jealousy. Secondly, the forty thought states of desire according to the *sPyod bsDus* are: attachment, lack of clarity, thorough lust, delight, medium delight, intense delight, rejoicing, strong joy, amazement, laughter, satisfaction, embracing, kissing, clasping, supporting, exertion, pride, engagement, helpfulness, strength, joy, joining in bliss, medium joining in bliss, intense joining in bliss, gracefulness, strong flirtation, hostility, virtue, lucidity, truth, nontruth, ascertainment, grasping, generosity, encouragement, bravery, shamelessness, perkiness, viciousness, unruliness, and strong deceitfulness. The seven thought states of delusion are, again according to the *sPyod bsDus*: medium desire, forgetfulness, confusion, speechlessness, weariness, laziness, and doubt.

Elaborate conduct (spros bcas kyi spyod pa). One of the various types of enhancement. Acts of procuring food and clothing, like a businessman, or keeping to detailed precepts and rituals.

Emancipation-gate of emptiness (rnam par thar pa'i sgo stong pa nyid). One of the "three gates of emancipation."

Emancipation-gate of marklessness (rnam par thar pa'i sgo mtshan ma med pa). One of the "three gates of emancipation."

Emancipation-gate of wishlessness (rnam par thar pa'i sgo smon pa med pa). One of the "three gates of emancipation."

Empowerment (dbang). The conferring of power or authorization to practice the Vajrayana teachings, the indispensable entrance door to tantric practice.

Ensuing perception (rjes snang). The perceptions or appearances perceived during the postmeditation state.

Ensuing understanding (rjes shes). The state of mind during the postmeditation state.

Essence Mahamudra (snying po'i phyag chen). The essential view of Mahamudra introduced directly and without being dependent upon philosophical reasoning: "Sutra Mahamudra," or yogic practices: "Mantra Mahamudra."

Essence of awareness (rig ngo). Same as the nature of mind.

Essence, nature and capacity (ngo bo rang bzhin thugs rje). The three aspects of the sugata-essence according to the Dzogchen system.

Essence, nature, and expression (gshis gdangs rtsal). The three aspects of the sugata-essence according to the Mahamudra system.

Essential nature of things (dngos po gshis kyi gnas lugs). *See* "suchness."

Eternalism (rtag lta). Belief in a permanent and causeless creator of everything. In particular, the belief that one's identity or consciousness has a concrete essence that is independent, everlasting and singular.

Ever-Excellent conduct (kun tu bzang po'i spyod pa).

Exaggeration and denigration (sgro btags + skur 'debs). Attaching existence or attributes to something, which does not have them + underestimating the existence or attributes of something that does have them.

Exhaustion of phenomena beyond concepts (chos zad blo 'das). The fourth of the four visions of Dzogchen. Same as complete and perfect enlightenment.

Expedient meaning (drang don). The teachings on conventional meaning designed to lead the practitioner to the "definitive meaning."

Experiences (nyams). Usually refers to the temporary experiences of bliss, clarity, and nonthought produced through meditation practice. Specifically, one of the three stages: intellectual understanding, experience, and realization.

Expression manifest in manifold ways (rtsal sna tshogs su snang ba). The third of the three aspects of sugata-essence according to Mahamudra: essence, nature, expression.

Extreme of eternalism (rtag mtha'). *See* "eternalism."

Extreme of nihilism (chad lta). *See* "nihilism."

Fabricated attributes (spros mtshan). Characteristics such as arising and ceasing, singularity or plurality, coming and going, permanence and annihilation, which are falsely attributed to the nature of things or to the sugata-essence.

First Dhyana (bsam gtan dang po). One of the four domains in the Realm of Form, the causes of which are produced through a meditation state of the same name.

Five bodhisattva paths (byang chub sems dpa'i lam lnga). *See* the "five paths."

Five elements (khams/ 'byung ba lnga). earth, water, fire, wind and space.

Five eyes (spyan lnga). The physical eye, the divine eye, eye of discriminating knowledge, the eye of Dharma, the eye of wisdom (also called "buddha-eye").

Five faculties (dbang po lnga). The five faculties "ruling" over the first two of the four aspects of ascertainment on the path of joining are: faith, zeal, mindfulness, concentration, and discriminating knowledge.

Five major root winds (rtsa ba'i rlung chen lnga). The winds circulating within the human body which have the nature of the five elements: the "life-upholding," the "downward-clearing," the "upward-moving," the "equally-abiding," and the "pervading" wind.

Five minor branch winds (yan lag gi lung phran lnga).

Five paths (lam lnga). The paths of accumulation, joining, seeing, cultivation and no-learning. The five paths cover the entire process from beginning Dharma practice to complete enlightenment.

Five powers (stobs lnga). Similar to the five "ruling" faculties but differing in that they have become indomitable by adverse factors. The last two of the four aspects of ascertainment on the path of joining.

Five skandhas (phung po lnga). The five aspects that comprise the physical and mental constituents of a sentient being: physical forms, sensations, conceptions, (mental) formations, and consciousnesses.

Five superknowledges (mngon shes lnga). The capacities for performing miracles, divine sight, divine hearing, recollection of former lives, and cognition of the minds of others.

Formless Realm (gzugs med kyi khams). The abode of an unenlightened being who has practiced the four absorptions. *See* "four formless realms."

Four applications of mindfulness (dran pa nye bar bzhag pa bzhi). Mindfulness of the body, sensations, mind, and phenomena. Their essence being discriminating knowledge concurrent with mindfulness, they are chiefly practiced on the lesser stage of the path of accumulation.

Four aspects of ascertainment (nges byed kyi yan lag bzhi). *See* the "four aspects of the path of joining."

Four aspects of the path of joining: Heat, summit, acceptance, and supreme attribute. For details see each individually.

Four domains of the Realm of Form (gzugs khams kyi gnas ris bzhi). The abodes of beings who have cultivated the meditative states of the "four dhyanas."

Four Formless Realms (gzugs med kyi khams bzhi). The four unenlightened meditative states of dwelling on the thoughts: Infinite Space, Infinite Consciousness, Nothing Whatsoever, and Neither presence Nor Absence [of conception].

Four formless spheres of finality (gzugs med kyi skye mched mu bzhi). *See* "Four Formless Realms."

Four joys (dga' bzhi). Joy, supreme joy, non-joy, and innate joy.

Four kayas (sku bzhi). The three kayas plus svabhavikakaya.

Four legs of miraculous action (rdzu 'phrul gyi rkang pa bzhi). Determination, discernment, diligence, and samadhi; perfected on the greater path of accumulation.

Four levels of emptiness (stong pa bzhi). Emptiness, special emptiness, great emptiness, universal emptiness.

Four right exertions (yang dag spong ba bzhi). To avoid giving rise to unvirtuous qualities, to abandon the ones that have arisen, to give rise to virtuous qualities, and to avoid letting the ones that have arisen degenerate. They are perfected on the medium stage of the path of accumulation.

Four sections of tantra (rgyud sde bzhi). Kriya, Charya, Yoga, and Anuttara Yoga.

Four visions of Dzogchen (rdzogs chen gyi snang ba bzhi). Four stages in Dzogchen practice: manifest dharmata, increased experience, awareness reaching fullness and exhaustion of concepts and phenomena.

Four yogas (rnal 'byor bzhi). Same as the "four yogas of Mahamudra."

Four Yogas of Mahamudra (phyag chen gyi rnal 'byor bzhi). Four stages in Mahamudra practice: One-pointedness, Simplicity, One Taste, and Nonmeditation.

Fourth empowerment of Mantra (sngags kyi dbang bzhi pa). Also called the "precious word empowerment" (tshig dbang rin po che), the purpose of which is to point out the nature of mind.

Forty thought states resulting from desire ('dod chags las byung ba'i rtog pa bzhi bcu). For a list, see "eighty inherent thought states."

Fruition Mahamudra ('bras bu phyag chen). The state of complete and perfect buddhahood.

Gampo Mountain (sgam po ri). Lord Gampopa's seat in Central Tibet.

Garuda (mkha' lding). The mythological bird, able to travel with a single movement of its wings, from one end of the universe to the other.

Gathering the accumulations (tshogs bsags pa). The virtuous practices of perfecting the "two accumulations" of merit and wisdom.

General ground of samsara and nirvana ('khor 'das kyi spyi gzhi).

General preliminaries (thun mong gi sngon 'gro). The four contemplations on precious human body, impermanence and death, cause and effect of karma, and the defects of samsara.

General Secret Mantra (gsang sngags spyi). The three first of the "four sections of tantra."

General vehicles (thun mong gi theg pa). Hinayana and Mahayana. Same as the "common vehicles."

God realms (lha ris). Six abodes of the gods of the Desire Realm; seventeen abodes of the gods of the Realm of Form, and four abodes of the gods of the Formless Realm.

Good Intelligence (legs pa'i blo gros). The ninth of the ten bhumis.

Gradual type (rim gyis pa). A practitioner taking the gradual approach to enlightenment.

Great Brahmin (bram ze chen po). *See* "Saraha."

Great darkness of beginningless time (thog med dus kyi mun pa chen po). Primordial ignorance perpetuated in the minds of sentient beings.

Great Pacifying River Tantra (zhi byed chu bo chen po'i rgyud).

Ground Mahamudra (gzhi phyag chen).

Group conduct (tshogs spyod). One of the numerous types of conduct.

Guhyagarbha Tantra (rgyud gsang ba snying po). The widely renowned Mahayoga tantra of the Early Translations.

Guhyamantra (gsang sngags). Synonymous with Vajrayana or tantric teachings. "Guhya" means secret, both concealed and self-secret. "Mantra" in this context means eminent, excellent or praiseworthy. Same as Secret Mantra.

Guru Rinpoche (gu ru rin po che). The Precious Master, refers to Padmakara, Padmasambhava.

Guru yoga (bla ma'i rnal 'byor). The practice of supplicating for the blessings and mingling the minds of an enlightened master with one's own mind. One of the special inner preliminaries.

Gyalwa Lorey (rgyal ba lo ras). A great master of the Drukpa Kagyu school. *See* "Lorepa."

Habitual tendencies (bag chags). Subtle inclinations imprinted in the all-ground consciousness.

Hard to Conquer (sbyang dka' ba). The fifth of the ten bhumis.

Heat (drod). The first of the "four aspects of ascertainment" on the path of joining. Getting close to the flame-like wisdom of the path of seeing by possessing concentration concurrent with discriminating knowledge.

Hinayana (theg pa dman pa). The vehicles focused on contemplation of the Four Noble Truths and the twelve links of dependent origination for the sake of individual liberation.

Ignorant aspect of the all-ground (kun gzhi ma rig pa'i cha). Synonymous with coemergent ignorance.

Inexhaustible adornment wheel of Body, Speech and Mind (sku gsung thugs mi zad pa rgyan gyi 'khor lo).

Infinite Consciousness. The second abode in the Formless Realm dwelling on the thought, "Consciousness is infinite!"

Infinite Space (nam mkha' mtha' yas). The first abode in the Formless Realm dwelling on the thought, "Space is infinite!"

Inseparability of the three kayas (sku gsum dbyer med).

Instantaneous type (cig car ba'i rigs). The type of person who does not need to go through progressive stages on the path.

Intellectual understanding (go ba). First step of three: Understanding, experience, and realization.

Joyous (rab tu dga' ba). The first of the ten bhumis.

Ka-Nying Shedrub Ling Monastery (bka' snying bshad sgrub gling). Tulku Chökyi Nyima Rinpoche's monastery in Boudhanath, Nepal. The name means "sanctuary for Kagyu and Nyingma teaching and practice."

Kaya (sku). "Body" in the sense of a body or embodiment of numerous qualities.

Kayas and wisdoms (sku dang ye shes). The four kayas and five wisdoms.

King of Samadhi Sutra (ting 'dzin rgyal po'i mdo). A sutra belonging to the third turning of the Wheel of the Dharma.

Lamdrey (lam 'bras). Path and Fruition/ Result. The main teaching of the Sakya school.

Lankavatara Sutra (lang kar gshegs pa'i mdo). A sutra of the third turning of the Wheel of the Dharma. Used as basis for Yogachara and Cittamatra.

Liberating instructions (grol byed kyi khrid). Oral instructions received from an authentic master which, when practiced, liberate one's mind from delusion.

Liberation (thar pa). Emancipation from samsaric existence.

Lord Dawö Zhonnu (rje zla 'od gzhon nu). Chandra-kumara, another of Gampopa's names.

Lord Gampopa (rje btsun sgam po pa). The father of all the Kagyu lineages. *See Life of Milarepa* and *Rain of Wisdom*, both Shambhala Publications.

Lorepa (lo ras pa). A great lineage master in the Drukpa Kagyu school.

Lotus of Nonattachment (ma chags pad ma). The twelfth bhumi.

Lower tantras of Mantra (sngags kyi rgyud sde 'og ma). The three sections of tantra: kriya, charya, and yoga.

Lower vehicles (theg pa 'og ma). Compared to Vajrayana, the lower are the vehicles of shravakas, pratyekabuddhas, and bodhisattvas.

Luminosities of mother and child ('od gsal ma bu). "Mother luminosity" is the buddha nature inherent in all beings. "Child luminosity" is the recognition of that which one's teacher points out.

Luminosity ('od gsal). Literally "free from the darkness of unknowing and endowed with the ability to know." The two aspects are "empty luminosity," like a clear open sky; and "manifest luminosity," such as five-colored lights, images, and so forth. Luminosity is a lucid wakefulness, the unformed nature present throughout all of samsara and nirvana.

Luminous wakefulness of dharmata (chos nyid 'od gsal gyi ye shes).

Machik Labdron (ma gcig lab sgron). The great female master who set down the Chö practice.

Mahasandhi (rdzogs pa chen po). Same as Dzogchen. Literally, "great perfection," the most direct practice for realizing one's buddha nature, according to the Nyingma, or Old School.

Mahayana (theg pa chen po). The vehicle of bodhisattvas striving for perfect enlightenment for the sake of all beings. For a detailed explanation, see Maitreya's *Abhisamayalamkara*.

Main part of practice (nyams len gyi dngos gzhi). Refers to the practice that follows the preliminaries: either yidam practice or, here, the actual practice of Mahamudra.

Maitreya (byams pa), the Loving One. The bodhisattva regent of Buddha Shakyamuni, presently residing in the Tushita heaven until he becomes the fifth buddha of this kalpa.

Manibhadra (nor bzang). A great bodhisattva of a past aeon.

Mantra Mahamudra (sngags kyi phyag chen). The Mahamudra practice connected to the Six Doctrines of Naropa. *See* Tulku Urgyen Rinpoche's Summary of Mahamudra.

Marks and signs (mtshan dpe). A perfect buddha's 32 major and 80 minor marks of excellence.

Means and knowledge (thabs dang shes rab, prajna and upaya). Generally, Buddhahood is attained by uniting the two aspects of means and knowledge, in Mahayana compassion and emptiness and in Vajrayana the stages of development and completion. According to the Kagyu schools in particular, these two aspects are the "path of means," referring to the Six Doctrines and the "path of liberation," referring to the actual practice of Mahamudra.

Meditation (sgom pa). In the context of Mahamudra practice, meditation "the act of growing accustomed" or "sustaining the continuity."

Meditation and postmeditation (mnyam bzhag dang rjes thob). "Meditation" here means resting in equanimity free from mental constructs. "Postmeditation" is when distracted from that state of equanimity.

Mental constructs (spros pa). Conceptual formulations.

Mind consciousness (yid kyi rnam par shes pa). According to Abhidharma, one of the eight consciousnesses. Its function is to discriminate and label things.

Mind-stream (sems rgyud). Individual continuity of cognition.

Miraculous powers (rdzu 'phrul).

Mundane dhyana ('jig rten pa'i bsam gtan). A meditation state characterized by attachment, especially to bliss, clarity and nonthought, and lacking insight into the emptiness of a self-entity.

Mundane samadhis ('jig rten pa'i ting nge 'dzin). Similar to "mundane dhyana."

Nagarjuna (klu grub). An Indian master of philosophy.

Nagi Gompa (na gi dgon pa). Tulku Urgyen Rinpoche's hermitage near Kathmandu.

Naked ordinary mind (tha mal gyi shes pa rjen pa).

Namo Mahamudraye (Skt.). Homage to Mahamudra, the Great Seal.

Naropa (na ro pa). The chief disciple of Tilopa and the guru of Marpa in the Kagyu lineage.

Natural face of dharmakaya (chos sku'i rang zhal).

Natural face of ground Mahamudra (gzhi phyag chen gyi rang zhal).

Natural face of mind (sems nyid rang zhal).

Neither Presence nor Absence [of conceptions] (['du shes] yod min med min). The third abode in the Formless Realm, dwelling on the thought "My perception is neither absent nor present!"

New Schools (gsar ma). The New Schools are Kagyu, Sakya, and Gelug.

Niguma (ni gu ma). A great female Indian master and a teacher of Khyungpo Naljor.

Nihilism (chad lta). Literally, "the view of discontinuance." The extreme view of nothingness: no rebirth or karmic effects, and the nonexistence of a mind after death.

Nine dhyanas of absorption (snyoms 'jug gi bsam gtan dgu). The four dhyanas, the four formless states, and the shravaka's samadhi of peace.

Nirmanakaya (sprul sku). "Emanation body." The third of the three kayas. The aspect of enlightenment that tames and can be perceived by ordinary beings.

Nirvana (mya ngan las 'das pa). The lesser nirvana refers to the liberation from cyclic existence attained by a Hinayana practitioner. When referring to a buddha, "nirvana" is the great non-dwelling state of enlightenment which falls neither into the extreme of samsaric existence nor into the passive state of cessation attained by an arhant.

Nonarising essence (gshis skye ba med pa).

Non-Buddhist extremists (mu stegs pa). Teachers of philosophy adhering to the limited views of eternalism or nihilism.

Nonconceptual wakefulness (rnam par mi rtog pa'i ye shes).

Nondistraction (g.yengs med). Not straying from the continuity of the practice.

Nonfabrication (bzo med).

Nonfixation ('dzin med). The state of not holding on to subject and object.

Nonmeditation (sgom med). The state of not holding on to an object meditated upon nor a subject who meditates. Also refers to the fourth stage of Mahamudra in which nothing further needs to be "meditated upon" or "cultivated."

Notes on Vital Points (gnad kyi zin tig). Scripture on Mahamudra.

Nothing Whatsoever (ci yang med pa). The third of the four formless realms in which one dwells on the thought, "Nothing whatsoever!"

Nyingma tradition (rnying lugs). The teachings brought to Tibet and translated chiefly during the reign of King Trisong Deutsen and in the following period up to Rinchen Sangpo.

Obscuration of dualistic knowledge (shes bya'i sgrib pa). The subtle obscuration of holding on to the concepts of subject, object and action.

Old and New Schools (rnying ma dang gsar ma). Although there were no new or old schools in India, these names refer to the early and later spread of the teachings in Tibet. Translations up to and including King Triral are called the Old School of Early Translations (snga 'gyur snying ma), and later ones are known as the New Schools of

Later Translations (phyi 'gyur gsar ma). Lochen Rinchen Sangpo (lo chen rin chen bzang po) is regarded as the first translator of the New Mantra School.

Old School of the Early Translations (snga 'gyur rnying ma). Same as "Nyingma tradition."

Omniscience (rnam mkhyen, thams cad mkhyen pa). Same as complete enlightenment or buddhahood.

One Taste (ro gcig). The third stage in the practice of Mahamudra.

One-pointedness (rtse gcig). The first stage in the practice of Mahamudra.

Paramita vehicle (phar phyin gyi theg pa). The Sutra system of the gradual path through the five paths and ten bhumis according to the Prajnaparamita scriptures.

Passing stains (glo bur gyi dri ma). The obscurations that are not intrinsic to the sugata-essence, like clouds are not inherent in the sky.

Path Mahamudra (lam phyag rgya chen po). The stage of approaching the recognition of the sugata-essence and of applying that recognition in one's practice.

Path of Accumulation (tshogs lam). The first of the five paths which emphasize the accumulation of merit, faith and mindfulness.

Path of Cultivation (sgom lam). The fourth of the five paths on which one cultivates and trains in the higher practices of a bodhisattva, especially the eight aspects of the path of noble beings.

Path of Fulfillment (mthar phyin pa'i lam). Same as the "path of no-learning."

Path of Joining (sbyor lam). The second of the five paths on which one grows closer to and joins with the realization of the truth of reality.

Paths of Learning (slob pa'i lam). The first four of the five paths on which concepts of progress, training and learning still remain.

Path of Liberation (grol lam). The path of Mahamudra practice.

Path of No-learning (mi slob pa'i lam). The fifth of the five paths and the state of complete and perfect enlightenment.

Path of Seeing (mthong lam). The third of the five paths, which is the attainment of the first bhumi, liberation from samsara and realization of the truth of reality.

Paths and bhumis (sa lam). The five paths and the ten bodhisattva levels.

Perfect buddhahood (rdzogs pa'i sangs rgyas). The extinction of all faults and obscurations and the perfection of all enlightened qualities.

Permanent or annihilated (rtag pa dang chad pa). Lasting forever as in an eternalistic point of view, or ceasing to exist as in a nihilistic view.

Personal experience (rang snang). Exemplified the dream experience, this term is sometimes translated as "one's own projection" or "self-display."

Personal manifestation (rang snang). Same as "personal experience."

Phenomena (chos, snang ba). Anything that can be experienced, thought of, or known.

Philosophical Schools (grub mtha'). The four Buddhist schools of thought: Vaibhashika, Sautrantika, Cittamatra, and Madhyamaka. The former two are Hinayana and the latter Mahayana.

Postmeditation (rjes thob). Generally, the period of involvement in sense perception and activities. Specifically, the time when distracted from the natural state of mind.

Practice Lineage (sgrub brgyud). The lineage of masters who emphasize is one's personal experience of the teachings as opposed to the scholastic lineage of expounding the scriptures (bshad brgyud). *See* Eight Practice Lineages.

Prajnaparamita (shes rab kyi pha rol tu phyin pa). "Transcendent knowledge." The Mahayana teachings on insight into emptiness, transcending the fixation of subject, object, and action.

Pratyekabuddha (rang sangs rgyas). "Solitarily Enlightened One." One who has reached perfection in the second Hinayana vehicle chiefly through contemplation on the twelve links of dependent origination in reverse order.

Precious Word Empowerment (tshig dbang rin po che). *See* "fourth empowerment."

Preliminaries (sngon 'gro). The general outer preliminaries are the Four Mind-Changings; the special inner preliminaries are the Four Times Hundred Thousand Practices of refuge and bodhichitta, Vajrasattva recitation, mandala offering, and guru yoga.

Purifying the obscurations (sgrib sbyong). The spiritual practices of clearing away what obscures the sugata-essence, example, the meditation and recitation of Vajrasattva according to the "special preliminaries."

Qualified master (bla ma mtshan nyid dang ldan pa). Someone with the correct view and genuine compassion.

Radiant ('od byed pa). The third of the ten bhumis.

Rainbow body ('ja' lus). At the time of death of a practitioner who has reached the exhaustion of all grasping and fixation, the five gross elements which form the physical body dissolve back into their essences, five-colored light. Sometimes the hair and the nails alone are left behind.

Realization (rtogs pa). The third stage in the sequence of understanding, experience, and realization.

Realized (mngon du gyur pa). The sixth of the ten bhumis.

Realizing the view (lta ba rtogs pa).

Realm of Form (gzugs kyi khams). Seventeen samsaric heavenly abodes consisting of the threefold four dhyana realms and the five pure abodes. The beings there have bodies of light, long lives and no painful sensations.

Resultant Secret Mantra ('bras bu gsang sngags). The Vajrayana system of taking the fruition as the path as opposed to the "causal philosophical vehicles." *See also* "Secret Mantra."

Ripening empowerments (smin byed kyi dbang). The Vajrayana empowerments which ripen one's being with the capacity to realize the four kayas.

Royal seat of dharmakaya (chos sku'i rgyal sa). Same as complete buddhahood.

Royal throne of the three kayas (sku gsum gyi btsan sa). Same as complete buddhahood.

Rupakaya (gzugs kyi sku). "Form body." A collective term for both sambhogakaya and nirmanakaya.

Sadaprarudita (rtag tu ngu). The "Ever-Weeping" bo-dhisattva of a past aeon used as an example for unwavering devotion and perseverance. He is mentioned in the *Prajnaparamita* scriptures.

Samadhi (ting nge 'dzin). "Adhering to continuity or evenness."

Samadhi of Courageous Movement (dpa' bar 'gro ba'i ting nge 'dzin). The surangama samadhi described in the Surangama Sutra.

Samadhi of Magical Illusion (sgyu 'phrul gyi ting nge 'dzin).

Samadhi of the First Dhyana (bsam gtan dang po'i ting nge 'dzin). *See* "first dhyana."

Samadhi of the Majestic Lion (seng ge bsgyings pa'i ting nge 'dzin). Described in the *Flower Adornment Sutra, Vol. III*, Shambhala Publications.

Samaya (dam tshig). The sacred pledge, precepts or commitment of Vajrayana practice. Many details exists, but the samayas essentially consist of outwardly, maintaining harmonious relationship. with the vajra master and one's Dharma friends and, inwardly, not straying from the continuity of the practice.

Sambhogakaya (longs spyod rdzogs pa'i sku). The "body of perfect enjoyment." Of the five kayas of fruition, this is the semi-manifest form of the buddhas endowed with the "five perfections" of perfect teacher, retinue, place, teaching and time which is perceptible only to bodhisattvas on the ten bhumis.

Sameness of space and wakefulness (dbyings dang ye shes mnyam pa nyid).

Samsara ('khor ba). "Cyclic existence," "vicious circle" or "round" of births and deaths. The state of ordinary sentient beings fettered by ignorance and dualistic perception, karma and disturbing emotions.

Samsara and nirvana ('khor 'das). Pure and impure phenomena.

Saraha (sa ra ha). One of the mahasiddhas of India and a master in the Mahamudra lineage.

Secret conduct (gsang ba'i spyod pa). One of the different types of conduct used as an enhancement practice.

Secret Mantra (gsang sngags, guhyamantra). Synonymous with Vajrayana. *See* Guhyamantra.

Seeing the mind-essence (sems ngo mthong ba).

Self-aware self- knowing (rang rig rang gsal).

Self-knowing mindfulness (rang gsal gyi dran pa).

Self-entity (rang bzhin). An inherently existent and independent entity of the individual self or of phenomena.

Self-existing natural flow (rang byung rang babs).

Self-existing self-knowing (rang byung rang gsal).

Self-existing wakefulness (rang byung ye shes). Basic wakefulness independent of intellectual constructs.

Seven aspects of union (kha sbyor yan lag bdun). The seven qualities of a sambhogakaya buddha: complete enjoyment, union, great bliss, absence of a self-nature, presence of compassion, being uninterrupted, and being unceasing.

Seven bodhi-factors (byang chub yan lag bdun). Samadhi, full discernment of phenomena, mindfulness, diligence, joy, pliancy, impartiality.

Seven thought states resulting from delusion (gti mug las byung ba'i rtog pa bdun). *See* list under "eighty inherent thought states."

Seven Wheels of Kshitigarbha Sutra (sa snying 'khor lo bdun gyi mdo).

Shamatha (zhi gnas) "calm abiding" or "remaining in quiescence" after the subsiding of thought activity, or the meditative practice of calming the mind in order to rest free from the disturbance of thought.

Shamatha cessation (zhi gnas 'gog pa).

Shamatha that delights the tathagatas (de bzhin gshegs dgyes/ dge'i zhi gnas). The shamatha state at the first bhumi which is embraced with insight into emptiness.

Shamatha with attributes (mtshan bcas zhi gnas).

Shamatha with support (zhi gnas rten bcas).

Shamatha without attributes (mtshan med zhi gnas).

Shamatha without support (zhi gnas rten med).

Shravaka (nyan thos). "Hearer" or "listener." The practitioners of the First Turning of the Wheel of the Dharma on the four noble truths.

Shravaka's samadhi of peace (nyan thos kyi zhi ba'i ting nge 'dzin).

Siddha (grub thob). "Accomplished one." Someone who has attained siddhi; an accomplished master.

Siddhi (dngos grub). "Accomplishment." Usually refers to the "supreme siddhi" of complete enlightenment, but can also mean the "common siddhis," eight mundane accomplishments.

Simplicity (spros bral). The second stage in the practice of Mahamudra.

Single circle of dharmakaya (chos sku thig le nyag cig).

Single sufficient jewel (nor bu gcig chog). The personal teacher regarded as the embodiment of the Three jewels, the Three Roots, and the Three Kayas.

Six classes of beings ('gro ba rigs drug). Gods, demi-gods, human beings, animals, hungry ghosts, and hell beings.

Six collections [of consciousness] ([rnam shes] tshogs drug). The five sense consciousnesses and the mind consciousness.

Six Doctrines of Naropa (chos drug). Tummo, illusory body, dream, luminosity, bardo, and phowa. *See* the "path of means."

Six Ornaments and the Two Supreme Ones (rgyan drug mchog gnyis). The six ornaments are Nagarjuna, Aryadeva, Asanga, Dignaga, Vasubhandu and Dharmakirti. The two supreme ones are Shakyaprabha and Gunaprabha.

Skandhas (phung po). Gathering or aggregation of many parts. *See* "five skandhas."

Skipping the grades type (thod rgal ba'i rigs).

Special preliminaries (thun min gyi sngon 'gro). Taking refuge, arousing bodhichitta, recitation and meditation of Vajrasattva, mandala offerings, and guru yoga.

Stainless (dri ma med pa). The second of the ten bhumis.

Stillness (gnas pa). Absence of thought activity and disturbing emotions, but with subtle fixation on this stillness.

Suchness (de bzhin nyid). Synonym for emptiness or the "nature of things," dharmata, it can also be used to describe the unity of dependent origination and emptiness.

Sugata-essence (bde gshegs snying po). The most common Sanskrit term for what in the West is known as "buddha nature", the enlightened essence inherent in sentient beings. It is also the aspect of the mind-essence present as the indivisibility of the two truths as itself the essence of buddhahood.

Sumeru (ri rab). The mountain in the center of the four continents. *See* "Meru."

Summit (rtse mo). One of the four aspects of ascertainment on the path of joining.

Superknowledges (mngon par shes pa). Usually refers to the five "higher perceptions" including clairvoyance, knowledge of other's minds etc.

Supreme Attribute (chos mchog). The fourth of the four aspects of ascertainment on the path of joining. The highest spiritual attainment within samsaric existence.

Supreme mundane quality ('jig rten chos mchog). Same as "supreme attribute."

Sutra (mdo). Discourse or teaching by the Buddha. Also refers to all the causal teachings that take the cause as whole the path.

Sutra and Tantra (mdo rgyud). Sutra refers to the teachings of both Hinayana and Mahayana. Tantra refers to Vajrayana. Sutra means taking the cause as path. Tantra means taking the result as path.

Sutra Mahamudra (mdo'i phyag chen). The Mahamudra system based on the prajnaparamita scriptures and emphasizing shamatha and vipashyana and the progressive journey through the five paths and ten bodhisattva bhumis.

Sutra system (mdo lugs). Refers in this context to the progressive bodhisattva path.

Svabhavikakaya (ngo bo nyid kyi sku). The "essence body." Sometimes counted as the fourth kaya, the unity of the first three.

Symbolic wisdom (dpe'i ye shes). The wisdom which is the unity of bliss and emptiness of the third empowerment and which is used to introduce the "true wisdom" of the fourth empowerment.

Tantra of the Two Segments (rgyud brtags pa gnyis pa). The short version of the Hevajra Tantra.

Tantra (rgyud). The Vajrayana teachings given by the Buddha in his sambhogakaya form. Literally "continuity," tantra means the buddha nature, the "tantra of the expressed meaning." Generally the extraordinary tantric scriptures that are exalted above the sutras, the "tantra of the expressing words." Can also refer to all the resultant teachings that take the result as the path as a whole.

Tantra of Directly Realizing (dgongs pa zang thal gyi rgyud). A tantric scripture concealed by Guru Rinpoche and revealed by Rigdzin Godem, the master who revealed the Jangter tradition of the Nyingma school. Contains the renowned "Aspiration of Samantabhadra."

Tantra of the Inconceivable Secret (gsang ba bsam gyis mi khyab pa'i rgyud). A tantra of the New schools which sets forth the system of Mahamudra.

Tathagata (de bzhin gshegs pa). "Thus-gone." Same as a fully enlightened buddha. The buddhas who have gone (gata) to the state of dharmata suchness (tatha). Synonym for "sugata" and "jina."

Temporary straying from the essence (gshis kyi 'phral shor).

Temporary straying from the path (lam gyi 'phral shor).

Temporary straying from the remedy (gnyen po 'phral shor).

Temporary straying into generalizing (rgyas 'debs 'phral shor).

Ten bhumis (sa bcu). The ten bodhisattva levels: The Joyous, the Stainless, the Radiant, the Brilliant, the Hard to Conquer, the Realized, the Reaching Far, the Unshakable, the Good Intelligence, and the Cloud of Dharma.

Thinking and stillness (gnas 'gyu). Presence and absence of thought activity.

Third empowerment (dbang gsum pa). The third of the four empowerments in the Anuttara Yoga system, which introduces the unity of bliss and emptiness.

Thirty-two thought states resulting from anger (zhe sdang las byung ba'i rtog pa so gsum). *See* list under the "eighty innate thought states."

Thought arising as meditation (rnam rtog bsgom du 'char ba).

Three gates of emancipation (rnam thar sgo gsum). Emptiness, signlessness, and wishlessness.

Three kayas (sku gsum). Dharmakaya, sambhogakaya and nirmanakaya. The three kayas as ground are "essence, nature, and expression," as path they are "bliss, clarity and nonthought," and as fruition they are the "three kayas of buddhahood."

Three kayas of buddhahood (sangs rgyas sku gsum). The dharmakaya is free from elaborate constructs and endowed with the "21 sets of enlightened qualities." Sambhogakaya is of the nature of light and endowed with the perfect major and minor marks perceptible only to bodhisattvas on the bhumis. The nirmanakaya manifests in forms perceptible to both pure and impure beings.

Three natures (rang bzhin gsum/ mtshan nyid gsum). The aspects of phenomena as set forth by the Chittamatra and Yogachara schools: the "imagined," the "dependent," and the "absolute." The imagined (kun brtags) is the two kinds of self-entity. The dependent (gzhan dbang) is the eight collections of consciousness. The absolute (yongs grub) is the empty nature of things, suchness.

Three realms (khams gsum). The samsaric realms of Desire, Form and Formlessness.

Threefold Purity ('khor gsum rnam dag). Absence of fixation on subject, object, and action.

Tilopa (ti lo pa). Indian mahasiddha, guru of Naropa and father of the Kagyu lineage.

Transcendent Knowledge (shes rab kyi pha rol tu phyin pa, prajnaparamita). Intelligence that transcends conceptual thinking.

Trekcho (khregs chod) "Cutting Through." One of the two main aspects of Dzogchen practice, the other being Tögal.

True all-ground of application (sbyor ba don gyi kun gzhi).

True wakefulness (don gyi ye shes). The wakefulness which is the unity of awareness and emptiness introduced through the fourth empowerment.

Tulku Urgyen Rinpoche (sprul sku u rgyan rin po che). A contemporary master of the Kagyu and Nyingma lineages, who lived at Nagi Gompa in Nepal.

Twelve times one hundred qualities (yon tan brgya phrag bcu gnyis). At the level of the first bodhisattva bhumi one is able to simultaneously manifest one hundred nirmanakayas for the benefit of beings. There are eleven other such sets of one hundred abilities. *See* the Abhisamayalamkara by Maitreya.

Two accumulations (tshogs gnyis). The accumulation of merit and of wisdom.

Two kayas (sku gnyis). Dharmakaya realized for the benefit of self and rupakaya manifested for the welfare of others.

Two rupakayas (gzugs sku gnyis). Sambhogakaya and nirmanakaya.

Twofold knowledge (mkhyen pa gnyis). The wakefulness of knowing the nature as it is and the wakefulness of perceiving all that exists. Knowledge of conventional and ultimate phenomena.

Twofold purity (dag pa gnyis). Inherent or primordial purity and the purity of having removed all temporary obscurations.

Udumvara flower, literally "especially eminent" or "supremely exalted," is said to appear and bloom only accompanying the appearance of a fully enlightened buddha.

Unchanging absolute ('gyur med yongs grub). Same as emptiness or suchness. *See also* "three natures."

Unconditioned dharmadhatu (chos dbyings 'dus ma byas).

Understanding, experience, and realization (go myong rtogs gsum). Intellectual comprehension, practical experience, and unchanging realization.

Unelaborate conduct (spros med kyi spyod pa). One of the various types of enhancement.

Unfabricated naturalness (ma bcos rang babs).

Unity of the two kayas (sku gnyis zung 'jug).

Universal Light (kun tu 'od). The eleventh bhumi and the state of buddhahood according to the Sutra system.

Unobstructed nature (gdangs dgag med). One of the three aspects of the sugata-essence according to Mahamudra: essence, nature and expression.

Unshakable (mi g.yo ba). The eighth of the ten bodhisattva bhumis.

Uttaratantra (rgyud bla ma). The "Unexcelled Continuity" by Maitreya. Published as "The Changeless Nature," Samye Ling, and as "Buddha Nature," Oral Teachings by Thrangu Rinpoche, Rangjung Yeshe Publications, 1988.

Vajra Holder (rdo rje 'chang). *See* "vajradhara."

Vajra vehicles (rdo rje theg pa). *See* "Vajrayana."

Vajra vehicles of the resultant Secret Mantra ('bras bu gsang sngags rdo rje theg pa). *See* "Secret Mantra."

Vajradhara (rdo rje 'chang). "Vajra-holder." The dharma-kaya buddha of the Sarma Schools. Can also refer to one's personal teacher of Vajrayana.

Vajralike samadhi (rdo rje lta bu'i ting nge 'dzin). The final stage of the tenth bhumi, which results in buddhahood.

Vajrasana (rdo rje gdan). The "diamond seat" under the Bodhi Tree in Bodhgaya where Buddha Shakyamuni attained enlightenment.

Vajrayana (rdo rje theg pa). The "vajra vehicle." The practices of taking the result as the path. Same as "Secret Mantra."

Vehicle (theg pa). The practice of a set of teachings which "carries" one to the level of fruition.

Very unelaborate conduct (shin tu spros med kyi spyod pa). A type of conduct for enhancement.

Victorious conduct (rnam rgyal gyi spyod pa). One of the numerous types of conduct.

Victorious ones (rgyal ba, jina). Same as buddhas.

Vidyadhara (rig 'dzin, knowledge-holder) one who holds (dhara) or upholds the wisdom of knowledge (vidya) mantra.

Vipashyana (lhag mthong). "Clear" or "wider seeing." One of the two main aspects of meditation practice, the other being shamatha.

Wakefulness of all existent objects of knowledge (shes bya ji snyed pa [mkhyen pa]'i ye shes). The aspects of the twofold knowledge which knows conventional phenomena.

Wakefulness of knowing the nature as it is (gnas lugs ji lta ba [gzigs pa]'i ye shes).

Wisdom essence of the tathagatas (de bzhin gshegs pa'i ye shes kyi snying po). Same as "sugata-essence."

Yoga of Nonmeditation (sgom med kyi rnal 'byor). The fourth of the four yogas of Mahamudra.

Yogachara (rnal 'byor spyod pa). The Mahayana school of philosophy established by Asanga.

Yogic practices ('khrul 'khor). Exercises utilized in the Six Doctrines of Naropa.

Zhijey (zhi byed). Pacifying, one of the Eight Practice Lineages brought to Tibet by Phadampa Sangye.

Masters and Texts Quoted in
The Heart of the Matter

Asanga (thogs med). Great Indian scholar; chiefly associated with the Mind Only School.

Buddha Avatamsaka Sutra (sangs rgyas phal po che). English title: *The Flower Adornment Sutra*, Shambhala Publ.

Cutting (gcod). One of the eight Practice Lineages of Tibet; connected to Machik Labdrön.

Dzogchen Hearing Lineage of Aro (rdzogs pa chen po a ro'i snyan brgyud). Focusing on the Mind Section of the Great Perfection; lineage transmitted through Aro Yeshe Jungney.

Gampopa (mnyam med sgam po pa). Early Kagyü master, disciple of Milarepa and teacher of the first Karmapa and Phagmo Drubpa. Author of

Golden Garland of Rulu (ru lu gser phreng).

Götsangpa, the conqueror (rgyal ba rgod tshang pa). 1189–1258. Early Drukpa Kagyü master.

Gyalsey Togmey Rinpoche (rgyal sras rin po che thogs med) 1295–1369. A great Kadampa master and author of the famous 37 *Practices of a Bodhisattva*. Also known as Ngülchu Togmey Zangpo (dngul chu thogs med bzang po).

Gyalwa Drigungpa (rgyal ba bri gung pa).

Hashang (hva shang). Chinese Mahayana teacher.

Khachö Lutreng (mkha' spyod klu 'phreng).

Kyobpa Rinpoche (skyobs pa rin pa che). 1143–1217. Early master in the Drigung Kagyü lineage.; disciple of Phagmo Drubpa.

Lalita Vistara (rgya cher rol pa, *Sutra of the Vast Display*). A biography of Buddha Shakyamuni. English title: *The Voice of the Buddha*, Dharma Publishing.

Lingje Repa (gling rje ras pa). 1128–88. Early Drukpa Kagyü master.

Luhipa, the siddha (grub thob lu hi pa). Indian mahasiddha.

Maitreya (byams pa). The bodhisattva disciple of Buddha Shakyamuni, teacher of Asanga and the next buddha to appear in this aeon.

Maitripa (mai tri pa). An Indian siddha in the Mahamudra lineage who was the guru of Naropa.

Manjushri ('jam dpal dbyangs). The bodhisattva disciple of Buddha Shakyamuni; personifying transcendent knowledge and the view of the Middle Way.

Marpa, lord (rje mar pa). 1012–1097. Founder of the Kagyü tradition in Tibet. Disciple of Naropa and teacher of Milarepa.

Milarepa (mi la ras pa). 1040–1123. The great Tibetan yogi; disciple of Marpa and teacher of Gampopa; known for his *Hundred Thousand Songs* and biography.

Nagarjuna (klu grub). Great Indian scholar; chiefly associated with the Middle Way School.

Naropa, the glorious (dpal na ro pa). Indian pandita, siddha and teacher of Marpa.

Noble Eight Thousand Verses ('phags pa brgyad stong pa). The middle length Prajnaparamita sutra.

Nyang Ben Tingdzin Zangpo (nyang ban ting 'dzin bzang po). Tibetan master; disciple of Vimalamitra and Padmasambhava.

Orgyenpa, the siddha (grub thob o rgyan pa). 1230–1309. A disciple of Gyalwa Götsangpa and the second Karmapa, Karma Pakshi.

Pacifying (zhi byed). One of the eight Practice Lineages in Tibet; connected to the Indian mahasiddha Padampa Sangye.

Phagmo Drubpa, the sugata (bde gshegs phag mo grub pa). 1110–70. Disciple of Gampopa.

Precious Master of Uddiyana (o rgyan rin po che). Padmasambhava; the great Lotus-Born guru; founder of Buddhism in Tibet.

Sakyapa, Lord (rje sa skya pa). 1182–1251. Also known as Sakya Pandita Kunga Gyaltsen; early master of the Sakya lineage.

Samantabhadra (kun tu bzang po). The dharmakaya buddha in the Dzogchen lineage.

Saraha (bram ze chen po sa ra ha). Indian mahasiddha in the Mahamudra lineage; famous for his songs.

Shang Rinpoche ('gro mgon zhang rin po che / zhang g.yu brag mgon po). 1123–1193. Founder of Tsalpa Kagyü.

Shavaripa (dpal sha wa ra). Indian master. Student of Nagarjuna and teacher of Maitripa.

Subhuti (rab 'byor). Among the ten chief shravaka attendants of Buddha Shakyamuni, the one famed for eminence in teaching emptiness.

Sutra of Nonorigination of Dharmas (chos 'byung ba med pa'i mdo).

Sutra of the Good Aeon (mdo sde bskal bzang). Dharma
Publishing.

Sutra of the King of Samadhi (ting 'dzin rgyal po'i mdo).
See also King of Samadhi, Thrangu Rinpoche, Rangjung
Yeshe Publ.

Sutra on Pure Intention (bsam pa dag pa'i mdo).

Tilopa (til li pa). Indian mahasiddha; teacher of Naropa.

Udana Varga (ched du brjod pa'i tshom). A Mahayana version of the Pali *Dammapada*.

Vimalamitra (dri med gshes gnyen). Indian pandita and
mahasiddha; one of three masters to bring Dzogchen
teachings to Tibet.

Yang-gönpa, the conqueror (rgyal ba yang dgon pa). 1213–
1287. Drukpa Kagyü master; disciple of Götsangpa.